It's the People:
Practical Lessons in Project Leadership and Stakeholder Management

Adrian Pagdin

AJP Consulting
2014

First Printing: 2014

ISBN 9780992907808

AJP Consulting
1 Dark Lane
Wargrave
Berkshire
RG10 8JX

www.ajpconsulting.org

Dedication

To Clare and Jerome for making sure it all made sense.

The Lessons in Leadership

Lesson 1. Get into bed with risk.

Lesson 2. Surround yourself with giants.

Lesson 3. Get a prescription.

Lesson 4. Hold up the umbrella.

Lesson 5. Look left and right before crossing the road.

Lesson 6. Get intimate with stakeholders.

Lesson 7. Clear the path.

Lesson 8. All stakeholders present and accounted for?

Lesson 9. Steer into the wind.

Lesson 10. Stand out from the crowd.

Lesson 11. See good, hear good, speak good.

Lesson 12. Be present in the present.

Lesson 13. Freeze and now relax.

Contents

Preface

I had an experience that you can perhaps relate to that involved travel, weather and delays.

I was on my way to Toulouse, home of the mighty Stade Toulousain, Airbus and EADS (the European Aeronautic Defence and Space Company) to deliver a talk on empathy. It was snowing a little in London but obviously there were far greater weather events happening across Europe as the departure board featured delays and cancellations to destinations across the continent. Eventually after an hour or so of ever retreating departure times an announcement came that we would indeed be departing but that the plane on which we were scheduled to depart had encountered some problems and that they were looking around to find a replacement. I can't remember the exact wording of this statement but it made me laugh to look out of the terminal window at the world's busiest international airport and hear words like, we are trying to find an airplane.

I made it to Toulouse where it was snowing heavily. As you land at Toulouse airport you can immediately see the presence of EADS with huge Beluga transport planes and even bigger hangars. I was struck that if only we could have arrived in our stricken Airbus instead of leaving it at Heathrow then surely they would have been able to fix it here.

The conference hotel was an hour's drive away and when I arrived, around 10pm it was a snowy, cold but brightly lit and festive scene. It was mid-November and in Toulouse snow is not normally expected until several weeks later.

www.ajpconsulting.org

This got me thinking about climate change and while unexpected snow flurries are not unusual I think that the jury is coming in with a verdict of positive evidence in favour of the changing climates on our planet. Everyone seems to be talking about it now, it's not just environmentalists but politicians and businessmen too. It's a big issue but with initiatives to reduce carbon emissions, the world seems to be taking steps to slow or stop the negative effects of our changing world.

Project, change and programme management is going through its own version of climate change. Since the late 1960s the development of change management expertise has delivered ever greater, more complex, more celebrated controls and methodologies. In 1971 the PMI (Project Management Institute) published the forerunner of the PMBoK[1]. The APM (Association of Project Managers) followed shortly after in 1974. Since that time the methodologies have multiplied, becoming more explicit and more exacting in the way that they respond to the central threats to change delivery: the unknown and uncertainty. I have worked with organisations that have developed risk logs that stretch to 30 columns, with PMOs (Project Management Offices) that employ reams of documentation, and with sponsors that insist on reports in Arial size 12 with a spacing of 14, precisely. In all of these cases I have also met change professionals who ignore the processes and the documentation.

It is as if for forty years we have become reliant upon methodology and control to deliver change. I have no beef with either, in fact they are essential. It is my opinion that while an over-reliance on methodology and control will not deliver consistent change benefits, the use of methodology and control *should* be seen as one of the many levers and approaches available to the change professional.

Change management is both an art and a science. Mostly I think that the art of the project manager is knowing when and how to apply the science. I'm not sure if this means that project managers are artists but there is an art form in integrating all of the processes and activities that go into a successful change initiative.

---

[1] The Project Management Body of Knowledge. A collection of processes ordered in groups and knowledge areas with practical tools and techniques to deliver change.

I recall designing a programme for a retail banking organisation that focused on developing core project management skills. Bob, one of the contributors, used an analogy which compared our aim with getting people playing sport well by providing them with the correct kit. Bob's sport was golf.

'Imagine that you arrive 100 yards from a hole that has a very small green area. You think about the shot that you want to play and then you decide which club to use. You might decide to chip and run with a nine iron or try and stop it with a wedge.'

The point is of course that you have a bag full of clubs, you know how to use them and you are able to employ the one that you feel will best suit the shot or the situation that is presented to you.

Have you ever watched professional golf? Players that earn millions of pounds a year will regularly refer to their caddy, to distance guides and to personal notes before selecting a club. Then, after a couple of trial swings they may even change the club because it doesn't feel right.

The purpose of this book is to provide the reader with a golf bag full of clubs; to provide tools and techniques that are presented as a reference and to act as a caddy. When you are faced with a particular situation you can turn to the appropriate section and remind yourself of the tools and techniques that could be applied and then select the most appropriate one.

In the following chapters I will present some research and articulate best practice. I will also share some of the many stories that I have heard and experienced over the past ten years. I don't have the monopoly on good ideas but I've met some inspiring individuals who are leading change not just in delivery but with their change teams. I'd like to share some of those ideas and to put leadership and interpersonal skills into the tool kits of every change professional, alongside methodology and control.

A note on the use of the words change, project and programme. I will refer throughout to the delivery of change and to change professionals rather than specifically to projects, project managers, programmes and programme managers. I believe that all projects and programmes deliver a change.

Introduction

My first proper project was to open the Holiday Inn Express hotel adjacent to the Nene Park Showground on the outskirts of Peterborough, England in the spring of 1998.

I remember the sense of excitement and anticipation with which I greeted the portable cabin on the edge of an acre of grass field.

The builders were to arrive shortly and construct an eighty-bedroom, premium economy hotel. My role was to:

o   Recruit and train staff.

o   Develop standard operating procedures.

o   Put in place marketing activities to attract clients.

o   Propose and agree pre-opening and operational budgets.

o   Procure and install all of the operational equipment required to welcome, accommodate and feed up to 200 people at a time.

My previous experience of such projects was limited to rebranding a hotel bar and managing functions, weddings and events. I had no formal project management training and very little support from my employers, who were wholly preoccupied in the land acquisitions that drove the expansion of these budget hotels through the nineties and noughties.

I know that I am not alone in my experience of plunging in at the deep end. Many of my contemporaries chuckle as they share similar stories of a fast learning curve, long hours and the thrill of the challenge. I've heard this referred to as delegation and stretching but I now recognise it as abdication.

I recall employing common sense and writing lots of lists. In fact the walls of both my portable cabin and my rented accommodation were covered with lists of tasks. As I learnt to incorporate lead times, deadlines and forward planning these became increasingly complex and sophisticated.

As the end of 1998 approached the hotel opened quietly but successfully. I think that it was resilience, curiosity and sheer determination that got that first hotel opened because I look back now and I recognise very little in the way of formal structure. Despite this, I had acquitted myself well and was rewarded with another hotel to open.

One year later, part way through project two, my curiosity was dulled, my resilience worn down and my determination blunted by the endless long hours and firefighting that I now associate with a lack of planning, control and senior management support. I was, as the Peter Principle would state, beyond my level of competence and I knew it.

I learned later that this was not an isolated case in the field of project and change management. In fact it is typical for individuals who excel in a technical area to be promoted to a project management role without the necessary training and support only to find themselves incompetent and increasingly frustrated. I'll expand on this in the chapter titled, The Effective Change Manager.

I was rescued by a friend who had a management position with a fast-growing telecommunications company, MCI WorldCom. I joined the company a few months before the Millennium as an organisational development consultant, tasked with developing standard operating procedures and training for the first line technical support call centre in London.

It's the People

Over the following few years I was to find out about structured methodology, controls, documentation, work packages, estimation, sequencing and Microsoft Project. I also had the tremendous fortune to spend time working with a group of experienced, talented and resourceful senior change managers.

I learned the importance of contracting success, planning realistically and delivering through people.

I had the opportunity to contribute to the development and deployment of a global project management methodology.

I was responsible for the design, development and implementation of a web-based CRM application for project managers.

I supported sales pitches and the subsequent delivery of technically challenging telecommunications networks for a range of clients including Bulgari, the London Stock Exchange, and Marks and Spencer, to name but a few.

In 2004 I set up my own project management practice and quickly found myself delivering a lot of training and organisational development workshops. It was through the workshops and consulting activities that I realised that my experiences as a developing project manager were not unique. I started developing ways to provide leaders and managers of change with tools and techniques and I came to love the impact that they had: helping people become better change agents and deliver real, lasting and welcomed benefits.

Over the past six years I have had the opportunity to work closely with some excellent companies and with some very competent, senior and successful change managers. I have worked on international initiatives like the ADWEA (Abu Dhabi Water and Electricity Authority) programme in the United Arab Emirates from 2008 to 2010. I have also worked with change management teams at varying stages of maturity.

I would note the retail and corporate change management teams at RBS (The Royal Bank of Scotland Group), the legal, risk and capital teams at Deutsche Bank, the change management teams at the Bank of England, programme managers at Xchanging and the leadership team at Greggs as being just some of the excellent opportunities that have allowed me to contribute to the development of effective business and organisational change.

I first decided to write this book in the winter of 2008 and started it in the summer of 2009. This book is based on my experiences as a project management professional and also on the experiences, war stories and anecdotes from participants on my workshops and those senior change managers who agreed to be interviewed.

It has taken me a long time to complete the book, every time I run a workshop I think of something else that I would like to incorporate, so I've put a stake in the sand and here it is.

Chapter One: Why Projects Fail

To understand how leadership can make the difference in change delivery, I feel it is important first, to understand some context. One of the first questions that we address on my workshops is, why do projects fail in your organisation?

This usually prompts an enthusiastic response as the participants share their war stories and capture a list on a flip chart page.

I would suggest to you that there are only three reasons for project failure and therefore three reasons why projects will enter jeopardy.

1. Late delivery (Time)

2. Over-budget (Cost)

3. Poor quality or not fit for purpose (Scope or Quality)

Technically a project has failed if it does not achieve the time, cost and quality criteria of the original objectives where those objectives have not been amended through change control[2].

Essentially when I talk about the reasons for projects failing I am referring to the triggers or events that will result in a project

---

[2] Many readers will recognise the reference here to the triple constraints and the scope triangle.

compromising one of the points of the agreed configuration of time, cost or quality.

The table laid out below represents the outcome of an experiment I conducted in 2012 that captured common reasons for failure from change professionals.

Trigger	% of respondents
Poor/Inadequate Project Communications	53%
Lacking Sponsor's Involvement/Ownership	49%
Scope Creep	39%
Poorly Defined Requirements	32%
Weak PM	21%
Lack of Control & Monitoring of Plan	21%
Absence of Risk Management	21%
Poor Stakeholder Management	18%
Poor Planning	18%
Poor or Weak Business Case	11%
PM Culture	11%
Poor HR Management	7%

Table 1. Reasons for project failure. Pagdin 2014

A research article by Dr John McManus and Dr Trevor Wood-Harper, published in www.bsc.org in June 2009 articulated the principal reasons for failure in IT projects that they had surveyed as being:

o A lack of formal stakeholder and risk management being factored in at an early stage and then as a result of organisational culture an inability to discuss issues, specifically stakeholder management, at project meetings.

o The lack of structure, skills, education or management discipline within the project organisation.

o A total reliance on methodology. Part of this reason was the lack of apparent leadership.

The OGC (Office for Government Commerce) states the following as reasons for project failure:

o The lack of a clear link between a project and an organisation's strategic priority.

o A lack of clear ownership and leadership at the senior management level.

o The lack of effective stakeholder management.

o A poor approach to project and risk management.

o Lacking skills to manage the project and risks.

o Insufficient detail at the breakdown stage.

o The lack of effective integration between supplier and customer project teams.

There are surely no surprises in these lists. Have you ever brainstormed or conducted a workshop to establish the challenges facing a particular initiative? If not you should try it. While there are unlikely to be triggers different to those on this list what it does illustrate are the challenges that are most pressing and related to the specific environments and organisational culture where the initiative is being delivered.

Prime Drivers

If you do conduct a brainstorming session to understand challenges and if you take that process to another level and try to establish root causes then you will start to see culture as a prime driver of failure.

"That's how it's done here."

Organisational culture plays a huge part in the success or failure of a project. If the organisation is aligned to change and project delivery then it will be a great deal easier than if it is aligned to production, delivery or BAU (business as usual). I have heard project management described as the business prevention department, I also recognise that for many organisations projects are seen as cost and not revenue centres.

At the heart of these arguments are organisational cultures. Understanding them is a big step in planning for successful change delivery.

"It's you," he says, levelling his finger squarely at the executive team. *"It's your fault that I couldn't deliver change. You wouldn't listen, you didn't support me and anyway, everyone knew that we didn't need this!"* Now there is some truth in this scenario, applied to many, many delivery situations where a conflict between the change team and the BAU or EXEC (Executive Committee) has caused tension and breakages. We will explore how to deal with these types of scenario later in the book but I want to pause a moment so that we can understand why organisational culture so often makes the delivery of change challenging.

A typical situation is where an organisation does not understand or support the unique culture of projects as opposed to business as usual activities.

o The need for up-front planning and time.

o The requirement to benchmark success clearly and in unambiguous terms.

o The understanding that a project has inherent risks resulting from uncertainty and the unknown.

o The difficulties in committing to firm time, cost and scope budgets while faced with novelty and complexity.

All of these conditions are at odds with the BAU challenges of performance improvement, efficiency, economy and achieving targets with products, services and processes that are relatively well-known, understood and embedded.

Throughout this book I will refer to case studies and examples. The ones that follow illustrate what can happen when an organisation's prime driver conflicts with project management.

Case Study 1: The Hubble Telescope

In 1990 NASA sent the Hubble telescope into space. The Hubble was funded in the 1970s with a proposed launch in 1983 but the project was beset by technical and budget difficulties, including the shuttle disaster in 1986.

When the Hubble was finally ready for operational use the scientists found that a vital part, the main mirror, had been incorrectly ground resulting in a severely compromised performance.

A remedial mission in 1993 finally resolved the issue and the Hubble has since provided the scientific community with a valuable asset.

In the case of the Hubble telescope, Charles Pellerin, NASA's Director of Astrophysics, the man responsible for putting the flawed telescope into space in the first place and the repairing of it states that the reasons for failure were contextual (Project Manager Today, September 2009). The organisational context created by NASA encouraged the principal contractor and manufacturer of the mirror, Perkin-Elmer to rationalise away the anomalies of the mirror and not report them to NASA.

This is an excellent example of where high calibre organisations with a commitment to highly technical engineered solutions can be subject to organisational bias.

In another example, one of my course delegates described a project that she had been working on for about a year.

Case Study 2: A Lack of Closure

The objective of the project was to provide all remote workers with mobile broadband through a USB or card-based modem.

The project had been ongoing for three years and had started out with a very high profile with a business manager being assigned responsibility. Over the first twelve months the project had lost its way as a result of neglected visibility and changing priorities. The second year had seen some successes and one team had been provided with modems, however the quality was poor. Users found the setup difficult and were critical.

The delegate was not the original project manager and was clearly struggling to make any headway. There was no clear budget, no sponsor and no sense of urgency. I asked what would happen if she did nothing with the project for a few months. *"Nothing,"* was the reply, no one really cared. Why had the project not been closed, I asked? The answers was that 'the organisation' rarely closed projects that could not be a demonstrable success.

For all of the controls and methodologies exacted by change managers, an initiative is heavily and negatively impacted if the culture of the organisation is not aligned to a structured project management approach. In this case the project could not have continued as it would have technically failed or been subject to high level managed change.

Another discussion, again with a course delegate, illustrated the point perfectly.

Case Study 3: Two Kinds of Support

I was asking how her projects were progressing. She responded with a wry smile and then went on to explain:

"I have two directors that I report to and I am conducting a project for each of them. The first director is a forceful character with a clear and vocal vision for his project to change the way that a business process reports data. The second is a much more laid-back individual who is hard to pin down on the finer details of exactly what success looks like in his project."

Progress on both of the projects was not without difficulty but with the former the project would be delivered on time, on budget and be fit for purpose. The director was driving the project relentlessly and, importantly, was very keen on documentation and process. Whenever there was an obstacle, the director sponsoring the project could be relied upon to remove it.

Conversely the second project was struggling to meet the deadline. The sponsoring director was hard to pin down, was uncomfortable with detailed documentation and was often surprised to hear that the project is not progressing well. When problems occurred, meetings were convened and the sponsor attempted to gain a consensus which often incurred compromise on previously agreed points of detail.

That these two diverse responses to the demands of projects were manifest within the same organisation is understandably frustrating for the project manager. It is not however, uncommon. Organisational culture breeds norms in behaviours that are then exported when individuals move to another company. These individuals, if in a position of reasonable autonomy then recreate the culture in their sphere of influence.

The beginning of this section is titled Prime Drivers. We can all relate to the fact that organisational cultures present challenges and that even within one organisation several sub cultures will exist. I have frequent conversations with change leaders about the prime drivers of resistance to change, conflict between the sales and service organisations, where today's income is prized disproportionately above initiatives to generate future incomes. In the subsequent chapters I will break down how to identify, understand and navigate individual cultures, preferences, wants and needs so as to create prime drivers for change.

It all started with a risk

What I have realised, teaching, coaching and advising diverse organisations is that the reasons for tension in delivering change can be predicted, managed and that they are organisationally specific. Take the following scenarios as examples:

o   In technology projects – the implementation of a new solution, the development of an application fix or migration to a new platform – these types of change have significant technology risks that must be overcome before considering implementation risks.

o   On the other hand, culture change projects that require individuals to change their way of working, cede responsibility or report differently will face complete failure or significant compromise if rejection occurs and so the likelihood of sufficient forces being brought to bear to assure acceptance must be established before considering subsequent risks.

o   When a business area has a reputation or track record for delivering highly compromised or tense outcomes then before exploring schedules, cost budgets, etcetera the potential for overcoming the underlying organisational fault lines should be established.

I strongly recommend that, whatever your preferred or prescribed approach to project management, you do a high level risk assessment at the earliest point. This is not the nuts and bolts, root and branch risk assessment that happens later, this is specifically identifying the big, show-stopping reasons not to proceed or strategy-defining conditions, organisational culture being a prime example. Practically speaking there are usually only a handful but getting them out in the clear and addressing them will either create the foundations for successful delivery or constitute a good reason not to proceed with the initiative.

Conclusion

I want to refer back to the table that I placed at the beginning of this chapter. The experiment was as a result of coming across a LinkedIn forum trail that was started off with the question, 'Can anyone give me some guidance about the main reasons for projects failing?' The contributor was new to project management and was interested in avoiding some of the known traps and pitfalls. I opened an excel spreadsheet and conducted a tally sheet to establish which reasons were most frequent. I kept going for about an hour and collected probably 75 to 80 responses. I was preparing for a tea break when a final comment caught my eye:

"I have been reading through your list of excuses and I have a question for you all; where was the project manager when all of these things were going wrong?"

I laughed out loud and enjoyed so much more my cup of tea. He's right isn't he, this commentator? Refer back to the list at the beginning of the chapter and ask yourself, which of these conditions could the change professional have managed, influenced, flagged?

I have spent this chapter drawing your attention to two facts:

o   That organisational culture presents us with real and pressing challenges.

o   That early identification of significant threats like organisational culture is beneficial.

However risks and threats have many faces, these challenges are part of delivering a novel, complex initiative into an organisation that must continue to operate in a sustainable and consistent way. It's our job, as the change professional to identify and overcome these challenges. In the next chapter we're going to dissect the effective change manager and explore some of the skills and qualities necessary to overcome challenges and deliver change.

It's outside the scope of this book to go into detail about risk management but as a project professional, it's our job to have a very high degree of intimacy with, and a tenacious attention to, the risks that stand in the way of successful delivery.

Lesson One:

Get into bed with risk.

Chapter Two: The Effective Change Manager

I recall arriving early for a conference where I was to deliver a keynote speech on the power of personal presence. I like to get to a venue early so that I can scout it out, walk the stage, try out the technology and establish an escape route. On this occasion as I walked up the stairs I saw a group of people wearing the same white tee shirts and being filmed shouting, 'Super project manager!' As it turns out they were, the conference was a huge success and I didn't have to use my escape route. Super project manager though, what does that mean?

Superprojectman enters the room. The board of directors look and nod approvingly. Superprojectman has big muscles to hold together all of the deliverables. He has x-ray vision to see hidden risks and threats and eliminate them. He has a brain twice the size of the average human to determine creative and powerful solutions. He speaks calmly, deliberately and smiles often, this makes others trust him and builds effective relationships.

Sadly Superprojectman does not exist. Instead we have regular project, programme and change managers who, where successful, capitalise on their strengths and augment their weaknesses with other team members.

So the question is, what makes an effective change manager? What are the prescribed strengths, attributes and characteristics?

I have learned that the skills and qualities of a change manager are generally the same across all organisations. However in the same way that organisational context places unique stresses on change initiatives, change managers in different industries and different companies have to call upon their skills and qualities in different combinations and measures. It's a bit like responding to the risks with the appropriate skills, on a project by project basis.

In this chapter I will expand on some research and draw some conclusions about how the effective change manager meets challenges by selecting from a bag full of skills, qualities, tools and techniques.

The table below represents a summary of hundreds of responses as to the skills and qualities of the effective change manager.

Skill or Quality	Frequency
Stakeholder management	90%
Leadership	85%
Communication	85%
Persuasion, influencing, negotiation	75%
Honesty	60%
Drive	60%
Questioning and challenging	50%
The ability to inspire	50%
Pragmatic	40%
Build and maintain an effective network	40%
Creative and innovative	40%
Accountable and responsible	30%

Table 2. The skills and qualities of an effective change manager.

Developing competence

As a follow on from the question, "Why do projects fail?" I almost always workshop the question, "What makes an effective change manager in your organisation?"

What becomes apparent is two facts.

1. There are definite skills and qualities that all organisations value, regardless of their level of maturity or industry type (like organisational skills, communication and the management of scope, time and cost).
2. In some organisations change management requires much more in the way of personal leadership, stakeholder management and communication skills than in other organisations where structure, control and frameworks assure compliance.

In organisations that have a mature projectised management approach (i.e. they recognise project management as necessary and a way of delivering business strategy) there is a greater weighting applied to stakeholder management, communication and the use of methodical controls. Whereas, in more operational organisations (where the level of governance is less apparent and perhaps projects are seen as cost centres, not contributing to income generation) there is a weighting towards relationship management, negotiating and persuasion. This difference is represented in Figure 1 on the following page.

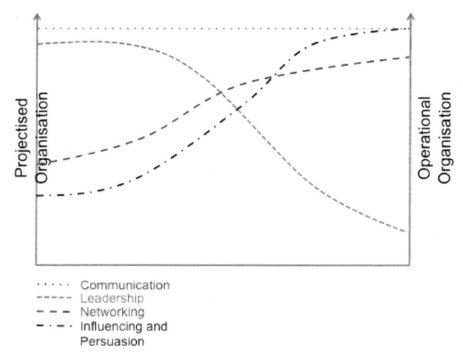

Fig. 1. Skills and qualities comparison.

The conclusion of this research is that organisational context places constraints on the way in which project management can be applied. The change managers that are successful across organisations are those that are able to flex their style, skills and techniques to match the environment.

Let's take a look at some case studies to elaborate further on the change professional reacting to the specific needs of the initiative.

Case Study 4: Remote Control Malfunction

I was told the story of a project to implement a procurement system for a UK government department that had a satellite operation in the United States capital, Washington, DC. This part of the MOD (Ministry of Defence) is responsible for procuring military hardware from their US counterparts and the driver was, as is often the case, to create greater transparency around spending.

30

The project involved a principal consultant whose role it was to design and implement the solution and a civil servant whose role it was to represent the needs of the department and project manage the initiative.

The principal consultant delegated the solution design to a third party.

The project started well with a research phase that defined what the London department wanted from the purchasing solution and what the benefits would be to the satellite location in Washington. Based on this research the third party consultancy designed a solution that exactly fitted the specification that had been agreed by the client.

When the solution was finally presented to the satellite location for testing, it became apparent that there were significant issues around fitness for purpose. For a start the language was British English whereas the larger part of the Washington administration teams were local. The backups of data were scheduled according to British time zones and created downtime during the middle of the US working day.

The issues were remedied but at a cost and the purchasing system was implemented one year late.

It is hard at first to understand what went wrong but it becomes more apparent when we examine the performance of the overall project manager. Here we find a very competent and experienced project manager, well-versed in delivering projects in a bureaucratic environment. He had set up a very structured project and had delivered everything that he had planned to do, according to very strict controls.

What he had failed to do was to ask the remote office what they needed in order to do their job or to understand the cultural context.

To understand how this happened we need to look at the wider organisational context of the public service. The bureaucratic context of this environment requires a very structured and controlling approach. The methodology Prince2 was designed to succeed in this context but not without flexibility.

In implementing this solution the PM had assumed that the compliant nature of the organisation in the UK was the same as that in the US and had failed to consult.

Case Study 5: Direct Action Damage

In direct contrast to the previous story I met a fearsome project manager while working for MCI WorldCom. She was well-known for her direct approach to achieving results through the strength of her personality and a superb network.

I had been with the company for a few months before, what was billed as, 'the inevitable phone call' came through to me in the first line technical support area.

'I want to know why the f**k the Deutsche Bank network has gone down.' Before I had the chance to answer this question the solid, challenging voice continued. 'What are you doing about it? I want to escalate this to Steve B' Escalation, particularly to Steve B who was then the head of the NOC (Network Operating Centre) and a third level escalation, was only possible one hour after a premium client had logged a fault.

When I attempted to manage the call in the normal way, taking down details of the symptoms, outage time and the like I was brutally brushed aside and then reminded of my lowly position in the organisation.

Looking back on that situation now it's funny but it wasn't at the time. She hung up on me and called Steve B directly, ultimately getting what she wanted: her client's network problem at the absolute front of the queue for resolution.

I was to come across the lady in question later on in my career and had the opportunity to spend some time with her.

To say that her clients loved her would be an understatement. It was like having a powerful and persistent gun dog in your pocket. Whatever the problem she would be able to resolve it quicker than anyone else, regardless of the agreed standard lead times.

The reason that this dynamic individual was able to achieve so much success was that she would bypass those processes and lead times that had been carefully negotiated to deliver a consistent service.

To understand such destructive behaviour we need to understand the history of both the individual and the company for which we both worked. Lead times and a sales-to-order process were

32

relatively new initiatives in a company that had grown from a market capitalisation of a few hundred million to billions in the space of a few short years. During this time of rapid growth the way to get things done was to be hands-on and in the absence of an order process to go directly to the individuals responsible for order processing, circuit design, provisioning and to beg, negotiate, bargain or threaten until your order got priority. This was a system that rewarded the bold and punished the meek.

This project manager was a creature of an organisational culture that had encouraged the type of behaviour that was now demonstrably destructive to those seeking to deliver consistent lead times through the process. That she had failed to adapt was not entirely her fault, to criticise her for doing what she had done so well and to such great acclaim for a long period of time would be unfair.

Quite often individuals find themselves promoted or moved to a leadership or management role without the formal training, coaching or support mechanisms to overcome the challenges of this new role. Without these mechanisms the individual can quite quickly become technically incompetent, unable to fulfil all or parts of the new role specification. In the case of the MOD PM there were some issues around underexposure to international working; with the WorldCom PM the issues were that previous cultural norms (at which she had excelled) were no longer acceptable.

The Peter Principle

Dr Laurence J. Peter and Raymond Hull in their 1969 book the 'Peter Principle' described how individuals are promoted based on their current competence and then beyond. Once beyond the level of competence the individual becomes incompetent.

There are many simple examples of this. Take a computer engineer who is employed to script code in a specific language.

Our engineer is very good. He responds well to the quiet environment and proves quicker and more effective than the peer group. Management recognise this fact by promoting our engineer to team leader.

Our engineer is not very inspired by this new role, however on a practical, day to day level very little has changed. The rest of the engineering team admire our engineer whose work is excellent and whose style is to get his head down and work. Performance is enhanced and there is a noted increase in motivation. The engineer's productivity dips though as he now has to attend meetings and write reports that take him away from his original area of competence.

Several months down the line and a significant business project is proposed to deliver new functionality to the organisation's application platform. Management discuss several project management candidates but settle on our engineer whose team will be central to the change.

Our engineer is required to produce some project documentation and estimate the duration of the project as well as costs. The direct team as well as subject matter experts and contributors from marketing, commercial, hosting and finance require him to direct and consult with them.

Unable to do any of these things well, our engineer immerses himself in the technical solution and specifically the coding. He neglects the commercial and marketing aspects of the project. He is seen to be reticent and uncommunicative by other subject matter experts. His own team starts to lose motivation as our engineer involves himself with the day to day coding, making changes and slowing down work.

After several months of negative feedback, senior management employ a consultant to analyse the project status. The consultant returns a verdict of non-existent communication, poor planning, no collaboration and overall poor project management. Our engineer is removed from the position and returned to the coding team with his reputation in tatters.

In this case the engineer was not provided with the tools, techniques or support to do the job. When he found himself incompetent he returned to his area of competence and comfort.

Another outcome of the Peter Principle is that individuals, when they have established feelings of incompetence, surround themselves with people less competent than themselves, or those willing to agree and not challenge. In this way they feel more comfortable. We call these 'silos of incompetence'.

The cocktail maker

In 1953 Neil Borden, in his American Marketing Association presidential address coined the phrase 'the marketing mix'. The phrase represented an idea that had been described by a colleague, James Culliton in 1948. Culliton saw the marketing manager as the 'mixer of ingredients' who sometimes follows the recipes of others and sometimes makes up his own recipes from existing or novel ingredients. In 1960 the concept of the four Ps was aligned to the marketing mix and prescribed four ingredients for the marketer to mix.

o   Product.

o   Price.

o   Promotion.

o   Place.

Over the past fifty years the four Ps have been augmented and now include:

o   People.

o   Programming.

o   Packaging.

o   Partnership.

The modern and effective change manager is also a mixer of ingredients. The recipes vary from organisation to organisation but the ingredients remain the same as those illustrated in Table 2 earlier.

As you read earlier, in some circumstances the change manager must compensate for a lack of formal governance by placing a greater emphasis on influencing, negotiation and persuasion. In organisations where project team members are co-opted from their day jobs the change manager may need to focus on the articulation of a vision, inspiring and motivating the team. Conversely in organisations that are highly projectised and feature robust governance the change manager must be able to effectively manage senior stakeholder and decision makers' expectations and to demonstrate highly-organised implementation plans.

As Neil, a senior change manager on a workshop once described:

"I completely embrace the requirement for up-front planning and the resultant reduction in risk but it's not an easy conversation to have with our senior managers. So what we do is we try to work in padding on the schedule while all the time tapping away at the governance structure trying to educate, influence and persuade."

"It does work, if you can demonstrate integrity and most importantly that there are benefits then management start to listen and then there's mutual trust. It takes time and a patient approach to stakeholder management while in the background working furiously to fix projects that are suffering from poor planning stress."

Flexing your style

In 1997 the car manufacturer Subaru won a hat trick of world rally championships with its Impreza STi WRX car. A huge feat considering the resources of the competition. However, the Subaru did not win all of the races. On twisty tarmac tracks, like the Rally of Sardinia the Subaru could not compete with the lightweight two-wheel drive cars, like the Peugeot and Citroen variants. Asked why this was the case, Paul Howarth of Prodrive (the company that prepared and raced the cars for Subaru) responded:

"If you want to build a car to win the rally of Sardinia then you build a two-wheel drive rally car, but if you want to build a car that can win the world rally championship, then you build a car like this (the Subaru Impreza)."

At the 2008 summer Olympic Games, cyclist Rebecca Romero became the first Briton and the second woman ever to win a medal in two different disciplines.

Her first medal, a silver at the 2004 Athens summer Olympic Games came from rowing in the quadruple scull.

She retired from rowing in 2005 after persistent back problems and took up cycling.

The individual pursuit event in which she won gold at Beijing has been dropped for subsequent Olympic Games and Rebecca is currently training to compete for the Olympic time trial event.

Conclusion

In the first chapter I said that your approach should be responsive to the project's risks. Building on that, I advocate that there is a need for the change manager not just to adapt the up-front approach but to be confident and competent enough to change their own approach throughout, identify others that can help and to build an effective change team.

I read that the famous investor Warren Buffet gives newly-promoted managers a matryoshka, a Russian doll. Wrapped around the smallest, final doll is a note that reads:

"If you want to build a company of midgets, employ people less able than yourself but if you want to build company of giants, employ people more able than yourself."

I like to believe that this is true because it's this foresight and humility that are at the heart of great leadership.

Lesson Two:

Surround yourself with giants.

Chapter Three: A Leadership Model

I have spent the previous two chapters looking at context: understanding some of the challenges that the change manager faces and understanding the diverse skills required to flexibly respond to the needs of the change initiative. I want to spend this chapter introducing you to a leadership model. The model is represented as a cycle and contains hanging actions that can be used and applied to different situations much in the same way as I referred to the need for the project manager to be the cocktail mixer in the previous chapter. Over the subsequent chapters I will delve into these leadership actions to provide illustrations and techniques for the toolkit.

The scope triangle

The scope triangle is dead. Long live the scope triangle!

The scope triangle represents the trade-offs and tensions that exist between these three aspects of delivering change:

o   Time.

o   Cost.

o   Quality or Scope.

Many commentators are now arguing that these original constraints are now insufficient and should be augmented with:

- o Environment.

- o People.

- o Organisational context.

Indeed in the latest version of the PMBoK the PMI has done away with the scope triangle arguing that the project has many more constraints to be observed than the triple constraints of time, cost and scope.

I was at a meeting of thought leaders where a new model was proposed that suggested that constraints should also include the vision, the rationale and the business benefits. Whatever the constraints that are specific to the project (I mentioned considering these in a risk-based approach in chapter one) the aim of the scope triangle as a model is to help change professionals apply appropriate controls to ensure that the constraints are managed, overcome or modified.

I developed the model below to illustrate the relationship between risk and control and to offer guidance on where and to what extent controls should be applied; perhaps you are familiar with the concept.

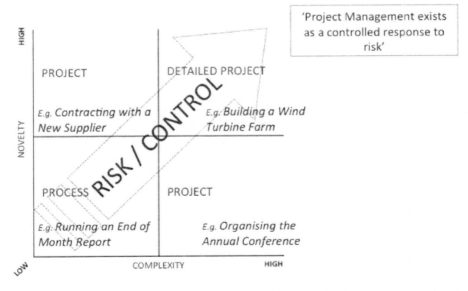

Fig. 2. The novelty and complexity model. Pagdin 2009.

The experienced change manager will apply those processes that are most appropriate to the level of risk and the level of control that the initiative requires.

In the next model, Figure 3, I have taken the novelty and complexity model and applied axes to represent the volume of stakeholders and the functional diversity, again perhaps you are familiar with the concept.

Fig. 3. Leadership complexity model. Pagdin 2010.

Leadership versus Management

There are many definitions of the difference between leadership and management. For the purposes of this book I want to use the following:

Management is about maintenance and leadership is about movement.

Within the context of change management, I will argue that once the plan has been signed off the change manager needs the management rigour to ensure that the plan is followed and delivered upon, that performance is maintained. The change manager also needs to demonstrate leadership so that the project team, the supporting stakeholders and the recipient business areas are prepared to follow the vision and accept the change.

In Figure 3 you will note that I have aligned management to a low degree of functional diversity and leadership to a high degree. It's impossible to avoid generalisation with a two by two matrix but the general implication is that an increase in functional diversity creates an increased load on the change professional to respond in a more tactical way and that more traditional stakeholder management models might prove inflexible.

The leadership cycle

What I propose is a leadership model that can be applied in the same way as other well-known project management methodologies. I have developed this model based on the conclusions of the previous chapter that illustrated the skills and qualities required of an effective change manager, i.e.

- o   Managing Stakeholders
- o   Managing Communication
- o   Inspiring and Persuading

The leadership model on the following page consists of five stages. Within each of the five stages are approaches that can be applied much in the same way as the processes in the project methodology stages. The change leader can select and deploy those leadership approaches that are most suited to the dynamics of the organisation or the situation.

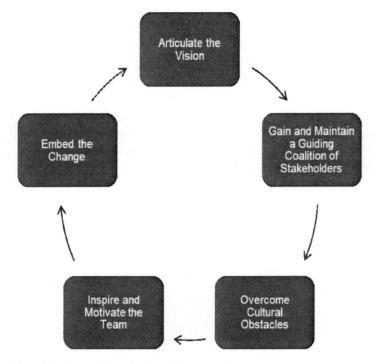

Fig. 4. The project leadership model.

For example, if the change leader is implementing a culture change initiative, such as a change in the way that people are managed, remunerated or measured then a 'bottom up' approach would be advocated. Selling the benefits, articulating the vision, getting buy-in from those that are going to be most affected by the change and those that can make the change difficult by either rejecting it or being adversely affected, these would be the actions that would have the most noticeable effect on success.

Leadership activities by stage

The next table describes the purpose and measures of success of the individual leadership activity groups.

Group	Purpose	Objective
Articulate the vision.	Ensure that there is a shared understanding of the brief and deliverables.	Contract the will and commitment to proceed with the change initiative.
Gain and maintain a guiding coalition of stakeholders.	To ensure that the stakeholder support required to complete the deliverables is accessible, appropriate and committed.	Stakeholders provide visual and vocal support for the change initiative at the appropriate points to ensure success.
Overcome cultural obstacles.	To remove the obstacles that stand in the way of success and to galvanise support.	Those impacted by the change are aligned to the change initiative so as to enable the desired outcome.
Inspire and motivate the team.	To achieve the necessary levels of buy-in and performance required to produce predictable deliverables.	The change team deliver the change deliverables in a predictable and collaborative way.
Embed the change / complete the phase.	To ensure that the deliverables are utilised in the way that delivers performance benefits.	The change / phase outcomes, service or result benefits the recipient organisation, and provides decision data to proceed or stop.

Table 3. Stages of leadership activity.

Let's take a look at an example.

Case Study 6: Digital TV switchover

In 2012 the UK television environment changed significantly. In a process that started in 2008, the existing analogue TV signals were converted to digital. Practically speaking this meant that unless your home television setup could receive and convert a digital signal then at a prescribed time between 2008 and 2012 you would no longer be able to watch television. Each transmitter in turn was switched over and users were given a short period to convert. One of the biggest challenges to the project team was apathy.

Ian was one of the programme managers responsible for introducing and measuring the performance of the new technology and then conducting the switchover. *"We can do the technology side without too much trouble, but a challenge is making sure that the public is sufficiently aware and enabled with the right information and options to ensure that they don't just benefit from the new technology but continue to watch television."* Ian explained.

For several years there had been a concerted television campaign declaring the benefits of the digital switchover. The digital tick logo was introduced to educate the public about what televisions are and are not compatible with the new signalling. There was even a personality – Digital Al – a silver robot that was chauffeured around the country to tell people that in the main, their current television will be just fine and there is nothing to worry about. These adverts started in 2007 and introduced Digital Al and the tune, 'Everybody's Talking' by Harry Nilsson. Every subsequent advert featured the music and Digital Al.

Still, despite the communication of the vision and the facts there remained the potential for the public to lose the ability to watch television when their transmitter was switched over. One of the initiatives in play was to flash up messages on television screens in the areas that were preparing to switch over. The message stated that the switchover was coming and could only be removed if the viewer actively pressed 'ok' on their remote control.

For the change leadership team, the challenges for this initiative were based around awareness and action from the public, not from stakeholders. The awareness campaign had three objectives:

1. Communicate a clear message that change is coming and that it is a positive one, a change that has benefits to all users; principally in terms of viewing quality and the range of channels available.

2. Educate the public about what technology is required to benefit from the digital signal and for those that must make a new purchase to remove anxieties about being taken advantage of by an unscrupulous retailer (the digital tick let the buyer know which TVs were suitable regardless of cost or functionality).

3. Finally, to communicate clearly that after a specific date the analogue signal will be switched off. Unless the required action is taken then the public will no longer be able to watch television.

The switchover to digital went smoothly, on time and with no negative technical or public issues. The awareness campaign was a significant contributor to that success.

This campaign featured two of the leadership life cycle stages:

1. Articulating the vision.

2. Overcoming cultural obstacles.

In the case of the UK digital TV switchover, it was not necessary to spend a great deal of leadership effort on gaining and maintaining a guiding coalition of (senior) stakeholders. The political and business will and mechanism was in place and contracted. It was also not a critical success factor to execute significant actions to embed the change. Once the switchover had happened the change would be complete. In change management speak, the alternative (a typical source of change stress) would have been removed. There is no possibility of the public not adopting the technology if they want to continue watching television. There are some activities in terms of leading and motivating the teams responsible for delivering the change but that was not seen as part of the main challenge.

Applying the leadership cycle.

Each of the five stages can be applied independently or in order at any stage of the project life cycle. As an example, at the startup and initiating phase of our life cycle, an initiative would benefit from an articulation of the vision that would galvanise the stakeholders whose participation and support would be required to overcome any cultural (or organisational) obstacles. The initial project team would then require the inspiration and motivation (as well as direction and guidance) to contribute to and complete the project initiation document. Finally with the phase approaching completion the organisational commitment would need solidifying and contracting, the change in mindset would then be embedded ready for the start of the next phase, directing and planning.

In the example below I have cited life cycle stages similar to the process groupings in the PMI's PMBoK. A life cycle does not need to subscribe to any specific model. It can be as simple as start, middle and end. But it is typically similar to the five phases stated in the table on the following page.

	Initiating	Plan	Execution	Control	Close
Articulate the vision.	Need to define clear and contracted objectives.	A robust and reliable plan to deliver a real benefit.	Restating the benefits and vision for change.	Restating the benefits and vision for change.	Completing effective lessons learned, developing skills.
Gain and maintain a guiding coalition.	Identify and contract with authorising stakeholders.	Enfranchise resource owners, maintain enthusiasm among authorising stakeholders.	Maintain support for the delivery through resource providers and power coalition.	Enfranchise the end user and recipient community. Maintain support from the guiding stakeholders.	Maintain support and commitment to the end.
Overcome cultural obstacles.	Opposing change initiatives, resistance to change.	Jealously guarded resources.	Overcome complexities and fatigue.	Manage end user expectations and assist with adoption.	Overcome fatigue, maintain commitment.
Inspire and motivate the team.	Create the necessary documents and manage expectations.	Create reliable and agreed plans and processes.	Ensure that deliverables are produced and performance maintained.	Deliverables are shown to be fit for purpose. Manage exceptions. Overcome fatigue.	Performance for the final deliverables. Provide feedback. Support the team as it disbands.
Embed the change / complete the phase	Create a sense of project and commitment to the objectives.	Ensure that commitment is given from contributing stakeholders.	All contributors form part of the project team and work towards shared goals.	The deliverables are adopted with enthusiasm and pragmatism.	The organisation learns lessons and commits to an evolution of change management.

Table 4. Leadership activity and the project life cycle phases.

As I proposed in chapter two, the change leader is a mixer of ingredients and a maker of recipes. Over the coming chapters we will look at these ingredients in more detail.

Conclusion

Most change professionals will be familiar with processes that can be repeated over the life cycle of a project. The fundamental and introductory courses that we run introduce the importance of applying stage controls and of initiating, planning, executing, controlling, measuring and managing life cycle stages. So it's not a great stretch to apply a leadership cycle in the same way, articulating the vision, gaining and maintaining a guiding coalition of stakeholders, overcoming cultural obstacles, inspiring and motivating the team and embedding the change / completing the phase.

At the beginning of this chapter I talked about constraints and the importance of applying change management in an appropriate way. The novelty-complexity and leadership models help to illustrate this fact. In the same way as I stressed the importance of an up-front risk assessment to guide initial actions then recognising that each change initiative will have a different prescription of processes, tools and techniques and leadership actions.

In the next five chapters I will dive deeper into these five life cycle stages.

Lesson Three:
Get a prescription.

Chapter Four: Articulating the Vision

This is the first step in the leadership life cycle for many change initiatives and from a leadership perspective it is one that can be often revisited to maintain a sense of direction, galvanise support and prepare the recipients for the outcome or get the team involved for the start of the next phase.

Case Study 7: Optical Illusion

The project had started well. The client, a prominent financial institution, had selected the vendor, a growing learning solutions provider, based on a winning combination of sound fundamentals and a radical blend of technology-enhanced learning and delivery methodology.

Tendering against the vendor had been a global consultancy and several well-known training organisations.

Three months later the project was failing. Failing to meet the expectations of the client and failing to maintain direction and progress even within the vendor organisation. Deliverables were being compromised as obstacles were put into the 'too difficult' box.

I asked the project manager what had happened.

"We started off with a vision of how this global programme would look. We were so excited to have won the pitch (perhaps unexpectedly) that we ran forwards at the expense of base-lining this vision with the client."

"We had a fractured vision but at the time we didn't know it because with our view of the project, things were going well. In hindsight there were signs that even within the delivery team we were not working towards the same shared vision. The internal communications were not great and there were early signs of frustration. However, projects are often like that at the beginning so we pressed on. I suppose it was something like an optical illusion because what we thought was going to happen was quite different from what the client was looking at."

"With just a few days to go before the vendor was to present the final design brief to the client there was a rushed meeting in the basement of a Costa coffee shop. The conflict was momentarily resolved as, finally, a vision and a mission were agreed. I say momentarily because again we failed to baseline this within the team or with the client."

The client presentation did not go well. At that time it became painfully clear that a failure to create a shared vision across the two organisations (client and delivery) had occurred. The client was agitated, confidence was impacted and costs had to be borne by the delivery organisation for the work to that date.

The project ended and the global programme went live at the beginning of 2011. I asked several members of the project team if it had been a success, something that they were proud of.

"Ultimately the programme will make money and in the long term, most of those involved will forget about the compromises, the issues and the long nights. So was it a success? Well against the core measure of delivering a profitable programme, then yes. Is it something that I am proud of, well no. The completed delivery methodology and technology-enhanced learning products that had been so radical and exciting at the beginning of the project were unrecognisable at the end," explained the principal consultant.

Articulating a vision is much more than completing a charter document; it sets the impetus, the drive and the urgency for an initiative. The vision provides the compelling need to keep going when obstacles rise up. The vision is the glue that holds the component deliverables together in a comprehensive and honest way, ensuring that the final outcome, product or service is fit for purpose. Something that the team could be proud of.

The purpose of articulating the vision is to ensure that there is a shared understanding of the brief and deliverables.

The objective is to contract the will and the commitment to proceed with the change initiative.

"The very essence of leadership is that you have to have a vision. It's got to be a vision that you articulate clearly and forcefully on every occasion."

--Theodore Hesburgh, President of the University of Notre Dame.

"Before you can inspire with emotion, you must be swamped with it yourself. Before you can move their tears, your own must flow. To convince them, you must yourself believe."

-- Winston Churchill.

An Effective Vision.

So what is an effective vision? I would say that a vision is a clear description of a future state where things are done better. I would also say that the true visionary is someone who does not describe a step by step instruction manual for recipients, rather they inspire actions in others by articulating a future state in such a way that others will strive to attain it.

A vision can galvanise actions that are exceptional. A truly effective vision is one that contributors and recipients not only buy into but feel part of; they aspire to own it.

Actions to articulate the vision:

- o Keep it simple.
- o Identify driving stakeholders.
- o Develop a sense of ownership of the vision by the senior stakeholders.
- o Communicate regularly in ways that are understandable by diverse stakeholder groups.

Deliverables to consider:

- o A high-level stakeholder map.
- o Terms of reference document.

- o Vision statement.

- o Problem / opportunity statement.

- o Business case.

The change leader can articulate the vision in different ways to different stakeholders.

Vision Examples.

"It's the economy, stupid!" This became one of the most famous election phrases and was used widely by Bill Clinton in his successful 1992 presidential campaign against George H. W. Bush. For a time Bush was considered unbeatable because of foreign policy developments such as the end of the cold war and the Persian Gulf War. The phrase, made popular by Clinton campaign strategist James Carville, refers to the notion that Clinton is a better candidate because Bush had not adequately addressed the economy, which had recently undergone a recession.

In 2003 MCI WorldCom consolidated its sprawling London offices into a new building in Reading, Berkshire. The business case was to create economies, financial savings and benefit from workers being co-located. The move was not popular, particularly as many people were based in the East of London. The vision for this project needed to be a compelling one that focused on benefits to the workers. In 2001 the company went on the road with a vision that stated, "The move to Reading will create a state of the art environment where our employees can come together, work together and create together." Of course there was no mention of commercial economies, the vision was intended to galvanise opinion and to create a desire to participate in the move.

In the 1970s and 1980s Hertz was the number one global rental company by some margin. Competing for a greater market share was Avis. They struggled to gain against the Hertz dominant position until they came up with a genius one-line slogan, "We're number two but we try harder"[3]. This slogan created a vision in the minds of employees and prospects alike.

Keep it simple

The vision must be simple to deliver, simple to understand and simple to access and be part of.

Clinton's successful campaign in 1992 and later Obama's successful campaign in 2008 were successful in part due to clear, compelling and simple visions.

- o "It's the economy, stupid."
- o "Change we can believe in."
- o "Yes we can."

These examples are particularly effective when you consider the historical backdrop. In 2008 the US had experienced the same president and governing party since January 2001. They had also experienced seven years of the 'war on terror' and large on the agenda was the collapsing housing market and the threat of a recession, brought on by the credit crunch of 2008. Against this backdrop it is simple to see why change was so compelling and something that 'we can believe in.'

There is a famous story about President John F. Kennedy's first visit to NASA's headquarters back in 1961. While touring the facility, the President's entourage reportedly came upon a man mopping the floor in one of the hallways. The President stopped to chat with the man, shook his hand, and asked what he did at NASA. The janitor proudly addressed the young President by saying, *"Sir, I'm helping to put a man on the moon!"*

This story illustrates the idea that everyone at NASA, regardless of his or her position, was in their own way contributing toward the ultimate vision and mission of the organisation.

---

[3] The story of the Hertz and Avis campaigns is detailed in the book, 'Positioning: The Battle For Your Mind', by Al Ries and Jack Trout.

The vision must be simple, understandable and believable.

If the change leader cannot clearly articulate the vision then it is unlikely that they will gain followers. A practical tip to create a vision statement is to write down all of the words that you can associate with the outcome of the initiative. Once you have a sheet of words, try to distil this list into as few, powerful words as possible and then link them together to create a statement. It's a bit like the funnel, reducing and refining to get to something powerful and meaningful.

I have illustrated this process in Figure 5, the vision funnel.

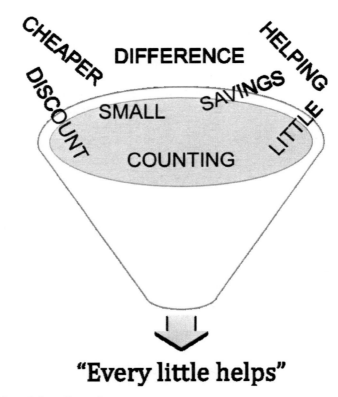

"Every little helps"

Fig. 5. The vision funnel

Identify driving stakeholders and foster ownership.

I hear the term, 'championing' a lot in my workshops. Simply stated, here are individuals who are constantly communicating the vision and the benefits so that when the change comes the business units affected by it are ready, they understand it and – we hope – they are receptive.

Case Study 8: Piggy Back

Neil was a senior change manager in a large European bank. His project involved large-scale behavioural change by literally thousands of people. The vision for change was a compelling one and the bank would benefit from the competitive edge that this change would bring them.

The challenge with the project was not a lack of clear business sense or organisational resources. The challenge was the context and the background of significant other change initiatives being delivered into the network.

"My project has been championed." Neil had managed to recruit a senior business leader to sponsor and promote the initiative. *"We needed a big voice and some clear air to ensure that the vision and the benefits were communicated, received, understood and desired by a very wide range of stakeholders, many of who were suffering from change fatigue."*

What Neil and his team did was to identify those stakeholders who had the most to gain from the project's outcomes and to engage with them in the early stages of the project.

"Even before we published a terms of reference document we started a communication campaign designed to get these senior stakeholders asking us questions. What we wanted to do was illustrate the problems. Bring them into stark relief so that the stakeholders' obvious question would be, what are we going to do about this?"

"The campaign didn't end there because what we wanted was for those senior stakeholders to feel a sense of ownership. We wanted it to be their idea. So we helped them to do that. Once they were on board things moved quickly. It was like a long and heavy freight train, there was no stopping it."

> Neil had employed a vision, successfully identified and contracted the main stakeholders, who then took up the role of championing the project at the highest level. They articulated the vision in the business and created the opportunity to communicate the vision and benefits.

It matters, the level of seniority, when it comes to delivering messages and communicating a vision. This is not always true, indeed revolutions often start as the result of a 'bottom up' uprising, however in most organisations, it matters. Access to the wider organisation, connections and networking at a high level, getting the right people in the room at the right time in the right mindset, it matters. It's not the responsibility of the senior supporter or champion to draft, craft and express the vision, it's their role to popularise it.

Communicate regularly.

I am going to refer back to the pioneering marketers that I discussed briefly at the end of the chapter two, the effective change leader. A definition from the Chartered Institute of Marketing, states that marketing is, "the management process responsible for identifying, anticipating and satisfying customer requirements profitably." Perhaps we can take a marketer's view when we are considering articulating the vision for change. Our definition of project marketing could be, "the management process for identifying, anticipating and satisfying stakeholder requirements and thereby achieve a successfully embedded change."

I like this parallel to the activities of the marketer because in fact, the challenges and activities that the change manager faces are very similar.

- o A competitive marketplace.
- o The need for a compelling call to action.
- o How to communicate directly and clearly with the target audience.
- o How to generate awareness, interest and desire so that the prospects will be compelled to act.

Case Study 9: Turning up the Heat in the Desert

A large state institution in Abu Dhabi, ADWEA (the Abu Dhabi Water and Electricity Authority) scheduled the introduction of a global development programme for first line management in 2011. The vision was to provide tools and techniques that would enable and empower the participants to take up their next, more senior positions with confidence and competence.

The programme was carefully designed with specific organisational insights and collaboration. Consultants from the provider worked with the employees, the target population, their managers, learning and development and learning providers to create a programme that was highly bespoke and featured simulations that reflected the type of challenges where the new skills, tools and techniques could be applied and add value.

Late in 2010 the pilots were completed with only minor issues and hailed as a success by the project's stakeholders, management and prospective delegate community alike.

The institution is growing fast and has tight targets to meet the expanding population and infrastructure of the state. The employees operated in a pressurised, demanding and highly monitored environment. Some of the comments, in respect of training, coming out from the community during the immersion research had been:

"Of course I value training but it's hard to fit in the time."

"If I'm honest. Unless I have to do it, it's unlikely that I would go on anything other than role-specific training."

"If I take two days out to go on a training course I will be working evenings and weekends to catch up. It's hard to justify."

In mitigation I'm talking about highly intelligent, motivated and capable individuals. The problem was that culturally, training took a back seat.

This training programme was not going to be mandatory so the challenge was to demonstrate that the management training workshops would be justifiable in terms of their value to the participant.

I had the opportunity to work with the very capable head of communications, responsible for the business area, who took this challenge in his stride and created a series of actions to successfully market the programme.

Background information was released into departmental newsletters.

Senior managers were kept appraised of progress and actively enfranchised into the process.

Departmental sponsors became responsible for certain elements of the programme (including design, monitoring, reporting).

In January 2011, launch events were carried out on consecutive weeks in Dubai, Abu Dhabi and Al Ain. Hundreds of prospective participants were invited to sample the look and feel of the programme and this was supported by high profile ADWEA figures.

The launch events were videoed and along with exit interviews consolidated into a short promotional clip that was distributed to the entire participant community.

Facts, instructions and messages articulating the benefits to the bank and to the individuals were sent to each prospect.

Each workshop was specifically tailored and designed to create a sense of fun and challenge. The objective of which was to generate desire in others to attend the workshops as well as creating a sense of anticipation for the next workshop.

Communication is just a word. It's an emotive word but on its own that's all it is. How, when, to whom, by whom – these are the things that make communication so effective and powerful.

Awareness, Interest, Desire, Action (AIDA)

Looking back at this case study, it's easy to see a marketing process in action. The acronym AIDA illustrates the series of steps that result in action by the prospect, in this case the participant registering and coming to the programme.

- o Awareness – background information, senior management involvement.

- o Interest – launch events, information packs and the video clip.

- o Desire – feedback from the workshops, the teaser video clip, benefits to the individual as well as the bank.

- o Action – booking on the first and then subsequent workshops.

Conclusion

There is a common theme to the successes of initiatives as diverse as the NASA mission to put a man on the moon, the campaigns to elect Bill Clinton and Barack Obama, and to gain market share in a dominated market and to successfully introduce culture change at ADWEA. In all of these cases the initiatives rallied behind a clear, compelling and believable vision that individuals bought into. In all of these cases the buy-in was sufficiently significant to achieve challenging objectives. In all of these cases there was a clear and compelling articulation of the vision, in the right way, by the right people that resulted in the right degree of buy in and support.

Lesson Four:

Hold high the umbrella.

Chapter Five: Gain and Maintain a Guiding Coalition of Stakeholders

Are you one of those lucky people for whom building effective and lasting relationships comes easily? Or are you like the rest of us who have to consider, plan and diligently work to achieve the same result?

Stakeholder management is a skill but it is also a process, a set of steps, that when followed carefully can and will help achieve the desired outcomes for your initiative and achieve the subtler ends through influencing and persuasion.

Step One: Identification

Step Two: Profile

Step Three: Segment

Step Four: Align

Step Five: Life cycle mapping and action planning

In the previous chapter, you read about the vision that can be created and articulated by the change leader and other champions to inform and create movement. In this chapter you will read about the second step, gaining and maintaining a guiding coalition of stakeholders. While this is articulated as a discreet step it is likely that the approach, tools and actions will be revisited throughout the change initiative life cycle to meet the changing membership of the guiding coalition.

Case Study 10: Standing in Line

Niall worked for a global telecommunications company. He was a project manager delivering data solutions across Europe. His biggest challenge was getting the right level of visibility for his project. This was how Niall described the change environment:

"There are some issues at play here. I make promises to customers, based on service level agreements but the business constantly fails to deliver and compromises. I recognise competing demands for resources and time, but I need to have the comfort that the organisation is behind me and will support me in getting my clients' projects completed on time, on budget and to the right quality."

The situation was one that will be familiar to many readers that have experienced an organisation's rapid growth and the failure of processes to match pace. The processes were not fit for purpose and so the users, the project managers, would short circuit the process. Instead of entering an order and allowing the process to govern its successful flow through the various departments, the project managers would actively engage with the individuals involved, asking favours and encouraging them to escalate and prioritise outside of the normal order. This results in an uneven playing field where consistency and reliability come second to the strength of relationships and networks.

I asked Niall what his objective was. *"It's not a difficult one to see,"* he explained. *"We need to have consistency and predictability so that as a community we can successfully make promises and manage the expectations of our clients. We need a process that works and a commitment to follow it."*

Niall's objective was to gain support for an initiative to change the process and create robust operating practices around it.

He goes on to describe his approach to managing stakeholders. *"I am not a natural networker and I find relationship building difficult. I started out by creating a stakeholder map and I considered what the reasons were for stakeholders not supporting me. My conclusions always came back to the same end; they did not feel that there was anything in it for them and they did not feel that supporting my initiative was the best use of their time."* So this was the first obstacle and consequently the first objective, to gain buy-in.

Niall then tells how he worked on articulating a vision to gain buy-in. *"I started working on compelling reasons why each of my senior supporters would want a project to succeed and I worked doubly hard to find something that was in it for them."* Niall was establishing the diverse nature of stakeholders' expectations and the need to manage them accordingly. *"One of the key supporters in getting all of my projects completed would be Order Management and the key issue for me would be getting my jobs completed at or before the agreed (committed) date. I considered that this department was unlikely to be happy with their performance against target and they were unlikely to enjoy the demands of 150 project managers clamouring for their unique initiatives."* So he prepared a brief presentation that supported the views of Order Management and in particular that, if every project manager followed the process of agreed service lead times and did not try to short circuit this with escalations, then committed lead times would be more likely to be achieved for the whole project management community.

Before circulating the presentation he had a brief chat with the head of Order Management and several of the OM administrators. They gave him their opinion and he was careful to listen to and incorporate their views.

I asked Niall if this had been successful as an initiative and this was his response: *"I would like to say that this changed the attitude of the PM community and that the demands on OM became more process-orientated but they did not."* He went on to say, *"However, two positive things did happen."*

"One, I rarely had to chase my orders through OM any more. Every time I called, the administrators remembered me and we would talk about their hobbies, challenges etc. In effect, I had created the right environment for relationships to grow."

"Two, I received very little in terms of feedback from my peers but one did stick in my mind. One of my peers came up to me shortly after and admitted that what I had done was perceived as politically motivated but that many of the other project managers had expressed a wish that they had thought of it first."

So was this initiative a failure? Against the objective of achieving a reliable and consistent delivery lead time through better process orientation, then yes, it failed. Against a background of resistance and conflict then the relationships and network that Niall had created was an impressive success.

When asking why this initiative failed it is moot to compare the circumstances with the initiatives discussed in the previous chapter. There was a general sense of frustration, not just felt by Niall but surely by all of the project managers who were subject to this broken process. Those individuals and their managers that were involved with and responsible for the delivery of service against agreed service level agreements would also be experiencing frustration as the measures would be demonstrating a failure to perform.

Niall articulated a vision for change but failed to gain sufficient support and momentum to gain momentum or reach the tipping point. In this chapter we are going to look at the process and activities to gain the buy-in and support from the right people at the right time and in the right way to make the vision into a mission and reality.

A guiding coalition of stakeholders.

Imagine having sponsorship at board level right at the beginning of the change initiative and that as a result the initiative was approved. Imagine then, that support being provided by senior leaders in design and production during the planning stage so that support was provided and resources secured for delivery. Factor in a commensurate degree of enthusiasm from those senior stakeholders that can provide support at execution, delivery and handover and you get an idea of the guiding coalition of stakeholders.

Actions to consider.

1. Identifying the full range of stakeholders able to positively or negatively influence the outcome.

2. Profile and understand the wants, needs, drivers and contribution of each stakeholder.

3. Segment the stakeholders into degrees of power and influence and map to different stages of the change life cycle.

4. Establish the position of stakeholders relevant to the objectives of the change initiative.

5. Prescribe actions to overcome obstacles, monitor and maintain support.

Deliverables to consider.

o   Stakeholder map.

o   Stakeholder management plan.

o   Power and influence chart.

o   Stakeholder bar chart.

Conclusion

Referring back to my comments at the beginning of this chapter, stakeholder management is in itself a process. It's a process that can be relied upon to do what processes do, produce a predictable outcome.

Over the coming pages I want to articulate the process and practical actions that can be taken to navigate between the steps, looking at some specific actions: identify, profile, segment, align, and life cycle mapping and action planning.

Chapter Six: Stakeholder Identification

A stakeholder is someone who has the potential to create a positive or negative influence on the change initiative. The stake is based on their perception of the impact of the initiative on them, their objectives or agenda. So with that in mind it's a fairly wide remit.

In the case of Obama's election campaign then, broadly speaking it was just about every interested person in the USA (and some that don't even know that they are interested).

The next case study certainly impacted on a lot of people, potentially every technology user in the world.

Case Study 11: The Millennium Bug

In the late nineties there was a lot of concern about the effects of the impending millennium on computers. The essence of this concern focused on the internal clocks in the computers. Apparently nobody knew what would happen when the practice of truncating the years into two digits (97, 98, 99) resulted in the number becoming 00.

This sparked a riot of activity with programmers that were previously redundant being asked to develop reserve systems using virtually obsolete programming languages. Systems that had been mothballed or forgotten about were fired up to be in place as back-up. There was a lot of talk about 'redundant contingency', which meant having numerous backup systems just in case. If the hawks were right then on January 1st 2000 it would not be possible to access your computer data, hotel check-in would have to be done manually, airplanes would not be able to fly without their sophisticated computer systems, the financial services system would grind to a halt and we would not be able to draw any money out nor pay bills.

At the time I was working for a telecoms giant in the centre of the city of London. I recall the sense of fear, excitement, adventure and anticipation as we waited for the fireworks both literal and metaphorical.

As I walked around the city on the eve of the millennium I can still recall the big banks and corporation buildings with satellite trucks parked outside, extra security, teams of IT 'experts' standing around drinking coffee. Huge amounts of redundant contingency in the event of the unknown.

Simon worked for one of the two prominent CRM application providers of the time. Lots of organisations took the opportunity of the upheaval to implement 'millennium' systems, applications that would allow them to successfully capitalise on a great new dawn!

"We were so busy in the two years running up to the millennium," Simon explained.

"It started off with a few of the investment banks and then, like a fire it started to spread and large numbers of organisations contracted us to implement Customer Relationship Management software applications."

"The basics of these applications are simple, their objective is to get the supplier closer to their customer through a more detailed understanding of their preferences." Simon then tells, *"But of course this had little to do with the current risk, which was the 'millennium bug'. The belief ran, however, that because what we were offering was high profile, enterprise and new and because it was being endorsed by senior partners in the consulting field that it would be immune (to the millennium bug)."*

The impact on organisational practices however, would be profound. A typical organisation, pre-CRM would be using a variety of systems to capture some or all of the necessary data: Excel, Access, Oracle databases, even white boards!

"What we were asking the end user to do was completely change the way in which they administered their data and forever change the landscape of their computer desktop," states Simon.

What happened at the beginning of the year 2000 is something that most of us will remember well. We came into work, switched on our computer (in some cases even the computers had been changed) and fired up a desktop that had changed.

The first to be impacted were the supervisors. Did they know that their applications were going to be changed? The managers knew but they had been totally engrossed with actions to mitigate the risk of the 'millennium bug' and hadn't fully communicated other system changes.

Then the IT helpdesks were inundated with calls that they were unable to manage. They knew about the new systems but were unable to deal with the sheer volume of contact. There were also serious concerns growing about the lack of a training facility.

In the end one of two things happened:

1. Organisations responded rapidly to provide training.

2. The applications were switched off and staff allowed to go back to their original state until a more structured implementation approach could be initiated.

Simon reflects back on that period, *"It's obvious now that we had failed to understand the impact on the end users and the power that they would then have. We had satisfied the needs and wants of all the stated stakeholders but we had failed to identify the end user community. The stakeholders that would ultimately make or break our handover."*

The biggest risk with stakeholder management is not poor management, it is neglect. If we fail to identify all of the initiative stakeholders we run the risk of them presenting obstacles, without adequate time to mitigate them. In chapter one I highlighted the impact of inadequate stakeholder support as one of the main reasons for projects failing; at the beginning of this chapter I have also stated that the process of gaining and maintaining a guiding coalition of stakeholders needs revisiting on a regular basis. It starts with the knowledge that the stakeholder community is not static, it grows and contracts and its membership changes throughout the project.

So how do we ensure that stakeholders are identified and engaged in a meaningful way?

Practical Tools

Some points to consider when identifying stakeholders:

o   Whose permission do I need?

o   Whose resources do I need?

o   Whose good will do I need?

o   Where will support come from at the various stages of the project life cycle?

o   Who will accept and use the output?

o   Who can negatively impact on the project?

o   Who will be impacted by the process, progress or the outcome of the initiative?

Consider the following tools / techniques

o   Mind mapping or brainstorming stakeholders.

o   Use an organisational chart and cross off unaffected groups.

o   Create a resource breakdown chart.

Using a mind map to identify stakeholders.

There are lots of different approaches to arrive at the end point of having captured all of the project's stakeholders on a map or chart. My starting point would always be to look for organisational process assets, existing maps or charts from similar recent initiatives, or to find organisational structure charts. It is easier to start with a global, pan-organisational view and make judgments about who is not involved than to create anew from the top down. Again, a point to bear in mind, that relates to my earlier comments, is that the process of stakeholder identification is not limited to the initiation stage of the project / process but throughout, from the start to the end of the project.

68

Figure 6 illustrates a stakeholder map, also referred to as the change professional's direction finder (looking upwards, downwards, forwards and backwards) deconstructing stakeholder groups into smaller parties. In Figure 7 the map goes a step further and illustrates individual stakeholders. Given that each of the stakeholders described in the illustration will have a different interest, the project team will need to plan different actions to effectively manage their expectations and keep them supportive.

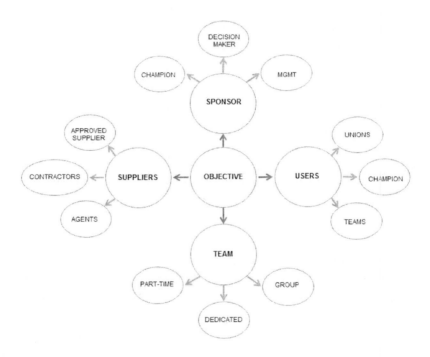

Fig. 6. A stakeholder map.

Fig. 7. Zooming in.

Conclusion

Stakeholder identification is not an activity to be undertaken by the change manager alone. One of the key responsibilities of the project sponsor is to maintain support and visibility for the project in the business. In another link to chapter one and chapter three, getting buy-in and ongoing support from the change initiative sponsor is vital throughout but very much so at this initial stage of stakeholder identification.

In the previous chapter you read about getting senior stakeholders to champion the project and articulate the vision, getting stakeholders to buy in to this 'sense of project' does not happen immediately. However, there is proof that early commitment is likely to be maintained. In his book 'Influence: The Psychology of Persuasion' Robert Cialdini explains that commitment can be very powerful and that once a small commitment has been given, if carefully managed this can be built upon and in fact, creates a barrier to exit.

At this very early stage, if you do get your stakeholders involved, a subtle change begins: the project ceases to be 'yours', it becomes 'ours' and if that happens then the level of commitment and support increases in line with the level of accountability that this degree of involvement brings.

Stakeholder identification happens throughout the life cycle of the initiative and stakeholders are present from inside, outside, the future and the past of the initiative as illustrated in the change professional's direction finder, Figure 6. It's often not the most challenging stakeholders that create problems but those that were not identified and therefore neglected. Stakeholders define and assure the project so be on the lookout: look left, right, up and down.

In the next chapter you are going to read about intimacy, getting to know the stakeholders in a way that enables the change team to engage and gain support.

Lesson Five:

Look left and right before crossing the road.

Chapter Seven: Profile Stakeholders

- o Paul is a senior director for a global retail bank. He will only read communications if they are presented in Arial font, size 10 with a spacing of 14.

- o Sarah runs a small startup and is on the go. She only reads emails that are sent with bullet points so that she can read them on her BlackBerry.

- o Martin is a decision maker for a media company. He will only read reports presented to him that are thin enough to get a staple through.

- o Belinda is the senior director in charge of customer projects for the European arm of a global telecommunications company. She requires that status reports are presented on appropriately coloured paper (Red for projects in jeopardy, Yellow for projects with issues and Green for projects on track)

What are your communication preferences?

Stakeholder management is a process that most of us navigate on a daily basis. For those of you that work in large organisational environments, you will be considering stakeholder management many times daily.

Simply put, stakeholder management is about obtaining a level of commitment that is sufficient for an initiative to succeed. The more that I know about my stakeholders the more able I will be to create an environment where my stakeholders will feel comfortable and will want to give me their commitment.

Dale Carnegie states in his excellent book, How To Win Friends And Influence People, *"there is only one way on God's earth to get someone to do something and that is to get them to want to do it."* The more I understand my stakeholders' preferences the easier it becomes to get them to want to support me.

My two and a half year old daughter rarely wanted to eat her dinner in preference for the pudding, so she would try anything to get around it.

She knew that her father was a soft touch for a cuddle so she would try crying and asking for a cuddle.

She also knew that if she ate her vegetables that mummy and daddy would be pleased and so she demonstrated the eating of a token piece of broccoli and then, after she had collected the praise say, *"Pudding?"*

At this early age my daughter was identifying and segmenting her parents as stakeholders in her initiative to have pudding without main course obligations.

Before I set out some ways to dissect and profile stakeholders, here is an example of successfully responding to stakeholder preferences.

Case Study 12: Turning "No" to "Yes"

Mark was a regional manager for a famous English bakery. He was sharing with the delegates on one of my courses the challenges he faced with a previous manager.

"This guy would just say no for the sake of it. Or that was how it seemed. Whatever proposal I would present he would say no, flat outright," Mark explained. *"As you can imagine this was frustrating and de-motivating. So I decided to do something about it and so I got a sheet of paper and I wrote down everything that I could about this man, his preferences, activities, his interests, his power base, motivations and ambitions."*

I asked Mark why he was doing this and he responded that he wanted to be able to understand why it was always a no!

"I identified a couple of things that I felt were important. Firstly he always liked to be seen to make the big decisions and secondly he was very vain about his appearance to senior managers," **Mark** goes on, *"I set off with a new strategy when I next needed the support of my manager to implement a new project. I asked if he could meet with me and when we did I started out sincerely apologising for causing him inconvenience, what with him being an extremely busy person. I suggested that the initiative would be unlikely to fly anyway and that I was probably wasting his time. I suggested that, perhaps, he had executives bothering him all of the time with initiatives that promised to deliver efficiencies, cost savings and profitability all the time."*

I can picture this scenario. For some of us this would seem high risk and I am sure that we all agree that influencing in this way requires really great execution. I can imagine feeling nervous at the idea of Mark's boss catching on to the fact that I was attempting to subtly influence him.

"Well as you can imagine," says **Mark**, *"he was taken aback and suspicious but I was prepared. I had been really sincere with my apologies and I knew that actually very few executives came with proposals because they would almost certainly be met with a flat rejection."*

"Well my boss, he then changed direction quite significantly. He assured me that it was no problem and that he was grateful that I had come to him. Of course he always had time for his executives and what was the idea that I had brought to him." Delighted with his progress **Mark** explains that he was keen to complete his strategy. *"I apologised for the incomplete nature of the proposal. I was certain that he would have thought of this already and maybe the best thing would be to leave it with him to consider overnight."*

Mark knew that the presentation was, in fact, well-researched and presented but Mark had shown his manager only two slides. The slides set out the benefits to the department and then how this would impact on the organisation as a whole, something very positive.

"The manager asked me a few questions about the supporting facts and then agreed to consider the matter over the afternoon. I thanked him for his time and his patience and then left." **Mark** explained the conclusion of the interaction. *"A few hours later, close to the end of play I was called back in the see the manager. He was very ebullient about the proposal. He wanted to be involved in it, to sponsor it and he wanted me to proceed to*

the next level. He thanked me for bringing it to his attention and even expressed a wish that more of his executives might come to him with similarly good ideas."

I asked Mark what he thought had happened and how this had affected his relationship with this boss.

"I suspect that he took the time between my leaving the office and the end of the day to take the presentation to his senior managers, perhaps packaging it as his and tested the waters before providing me with the go decision. Since that moment I have been careful to manage his expectations but he has never turned down a sound business case since, at least not from me!"

What Mark did was to profile his stakeholder. We are all influenced by our preferences and those who seek to gain our trust, support or buy-in will be well advised to understand those preferences. I started off this chapter describing some diverse preferences that I have learned during my years as a coach and facilitator. I often ask change leaders how they would respond if they had four senior stakeholders, all of whom required their expectations to be well-managed (in return for support) and further, if those four senior manages had completely different communication preferences. Would you format your presentation four times? Conduct a face to face presentation or one and prepare a detailed report for another? The answer is a qualified yes. Yes, if you needed buy-in and support.

What Mark did was to profile his stakeholder and then based on his understanding of his boss' preferences he radically altered his approach. In this case Mark successfully achieved his primary objective, he got the proposal approved, but he achieved something more significant, he achieved a degree of trust and commitment from his boss. The barriers to support had been lowered for the future.

We might never agree completely with the preferences, the drivers of our stakeholders, but it is we who must adapt our behaviour to manage their expectations, if their support and buy-in is essential.

I have mentioned already how stakeholder management is a repeatable process. In the following example, Phillipa explains how she achieves her goal and a win-win outcome through applying a process that includes understanding and profiling her stakeholders.

Case Study 13: Influencing Stakeholders

Phillipa would like to take two weeks' family holiday in the middle of August. Phillipa recognises that this is peak family holiday time and that other members of the team will also want time off during this period.

Phillipa will need a commitment from her manager and to get this she will need to demonstrate that the team will not be left short and that there is no clash between her holiday wants and those of another team members.

"I don't think of this as stakeholder management. It's just common sense," Phillipa begins. *"I know that Mark (the manager) wants team harmony and for the team to have no more than one team member off at a time, to ensure that the department functions well in my absence."*

"So I try to discuss holidays with my team mates in advance. I identify what I want in advance, as early as possible, usually around February. What I try to do is appear flexible and accommodating so I present it to my team mates as their choice."

"It is rare that anyone is as organised as me so early on and so usually there is no conflict. There are eight weeks of school holidays and only three of us with children in school. So there shouldn't be any issues, but I want to get the matter resolved early and ensure that there is no ill will."

"If I go into work and state that I will be booking my holidays between x dates then I am likely to attract criticism. The fact is everyone likes to be consulted so I ask each of my team members what their holiday commitments are. I say that I don't mind when mine are. In fact, I get to choose my dates every year!"

"Because I am being so flexible and I am giving my colleagues the choice, they always defer and say that they don't mind. I have almost always got the dates that I want without conflict and while projecting that I am a considerate, flexible team member."

Phillipa has followed a process that identifies the needs and wants of her fellow workers and her boss and then created what appears to all stakeholders as a win-win situation. In this example, careful planning, expectations management and a good understanding of the preferences of the other stakeholders has created a genuinely positive outcome.

The final example deals with the importance of clearly and correctly defining expectations. I define expectations as "what's in this for me?"

Case Study 14: The Power of Reputation.

In 2001 when companies were becoming very excited about the concept of centralised customer relationship management applications, on the ground the reality was often lots of Excel-based spreadsheets that maintained all sorts of project and operational performance data.

One such organisation, Telco, had grown rapidly and was a contender for Europe's foremost communications company with the ability to manage data in most European countries. With up to 200 client projects being delivered at any one time, maintaining an overview of project performance, resource optimisation and reporting was time consuming and labour intensive. A project was initiated to reduce the time spent, increase the speed to access up to date information and create a portal where PMs could log in and update progress in real time.

The tender process came down to two providers, both of whom were proposing a web-based solution. This was starkly different to the machine-based applications (like Excel) that relied upon centralised co-ordination and aggregation. The two tenders were also very different in their approach and costing.

Option one involved engaging a consultancy that defined a clear set of steps to discover, define and then build what was a ground-up concept. The company was established and put forwards clear terms of engagement and a clear view of the development path.

Option two involved a much smaller organisation, essentially a two-man startup who were struggling to articulate the design steps but were extremely confident and enthusiastic about the project.

What became clear was that while there was a clear distinction between the established provider and the newcomer in terms of process predictability, the fundamental scope risk remained the same, that what we wanted had not been done before and might not work. What the Telco organisation needed was a partner that could be relied upon to work closely with them throughout development and beyond. What was also apparent was that, while the two-man start-up would require support from the client to manage the process their approach, enthusiasm and their cost-proposal was much more attractive. What finally settled the decision, however, was the fact that the startup company needed a positive outcome as much as the client Telco did.

Throughout 2001 and 2002 the supplier put in a huge effort, far beyond their initial cost estimate and without any additional financial payment to develop an elegant and fully functional web-based project management reporting and database application. The fact that this successful outcome was achieved was certainly down to good communication and clear goals but fundamentally was built on a clear alignment of organisational expectations. For both parties the final outcome and its success was pivotal. For the supplier, the reference formed the foundation of future successes and for the client it provided the benchmark for effective reporting and the vehicle for enhanced project delivery performance.

It is overly simple to assume that suppliers, contractors and staff are motivated purely by financial gain. The focus of understanding stakeholders is to dig beneath the traditional bias and to find drivers that can be used to leverage something other than compliance.

o Users may not see the benefits of a new application but they may see the benefits of making that new application as simple to use and as hassle-free for them to move over to.

o A resource manager may be obliged to help populate a staffing plan but they may be inclined to help more if their preferences are catered to and if they are sincerely thanked.

o A senior stakeholder may be identified as the project sponsor but their full engagement and support may only be secured once the benefits to them and their personal reputation have been carefully articulated.

Stakeholder profiling is about identifying the levers that can be used to enhance performance and create a win-win situation.

Stakeholder Preferences

Some points to consider when identifying stakeholder preferences:

o   Communication styles (when, by whom, in what format, what information and why).

o   Agenda (What do they really want to see happening and is this different from their stated position?)

o   Expectations (What do they want from the project and from the project manager?)

o   Motivation.

o   Power / Influence (To what degree can they positively or negatively influence the outcome, or the progress of the initiative?)

o   Contribution (what is their role in the initiative?)

Practical tools to consider:

o   Identify and execute a win-win strategy.

o   Consult with peers to understand the bias and performance of stakeholders.

o   Speak to stakeholders directly and ask them what they want and when.

The win-win situation.

In 1964, Victor Vroom articulated his theory of expectancy. The theory has three formulae:

1.   Expectancy, the achievement of a desired level of performance.

2.   Instrumentality, that actions will attract reward.

3.   Valence, the value of the rewards weighed against personal needs and situation.

Vroom's expectancy theory has been widely accepted as explaining how individuals choose from behavioural options. In making a decision an individual is weighing up personal benefits.

When profiling stakeholders there can be a simple exchange required, based upon the stakeholder performing a service for the benefit of the change initiative to a prescribed degree of performance, in return for which the stakeholder has an expectation that they will receive something in return.

If we consider this exchange from the perspective of Vroom's theory then the levers that we are seeking to understand are those that will demonstrate expectancy, instrumentality or valence.

For example, it might be my job to process project invoices and as a customer, the project manager can expect a reasonable level of service but let's say that we require the supplier (the invoice processing clerk) to expedite this piece of work or to complete it in a different way, perhaps involving going above and beyond their job description. How can we encourage the individual to behave positively when they do not have to?

I propose that by understanding personal preferences, drivers, motivators and needs we are better placed to apply the right levers and create:

1. A situation where the individual feels positive about their performance (expectancy)

2. A situation where the individual feels the reward is commensurate with the effort (instrumentality)

3. A situation where the reward is specific to that individual's value and needs system (valence)

Table 5 provides an example of this simple exchange, identifying a strategy to leverage interest to obtain contribution.

Stakeholder	Contribution	Interest	Strategy
Client PM	Collaboration	Internal perception of successful project	Market the successes of the project internally
Order Management Clerk	On time processing	An easy life	Demonstrate the simplicity of the requests

Table 5. Managing expectations.

Stakeholder dictionary

A technique that illustrates the win-win situation and also leverages what is known about stakeholders in organisational process assets (previous documentation) and enterprise environmental factors (personal experiences) is to define stakeholders in more detail and create a stakeholder dictionary.

This is a technique that is best employed with a small team of supporters, the change team or professionals with stakeholder insights.

Using the stakeholder register as a starting point, describe:

o What is in it for this stakeholder, what is their want, ambition, need, expectation?

o What does the change initiative want or need from this stakeholder?

These two initial pieces of information, if accurate, create the foundation for an initial transactional exchange.

Conclusion

When we work in teams for long periods of time we find that we get to know each other's preferences and to some extent, we start to make allowances. These allowances are the normalisation step required to move on to a higher level of team performance. In a project environment, there is often very little time available to get to know people and plenty of opportunities to misread or misjudge resulting in frustration and conflict.

By focusing on identifying the personalities of our stakeholders through previous experience (previous actions are the best predictor of future behaviour), research and observation the project leader can accelerate the process of normalisation in the temporary team and reduce the likelihood and the frequency of stakeholder frustration and conflict.

Lesson Six:

Get intimate with stakeholders.

Chapter Eight: The Stakeholder Bar Chart

In chapter seven, you read about the importance of getting to know stakeholders with the aim of being able to engage with them and have meaningful conversations. In this chapter we will explore when to engage and when to have the meaningful conversations to greatest effect.

How many emails a day do you get? I receive a modest 40 to 50. I understand that some people receive hundreds a day. To remain sane and productive it is necessary to prioritise these emails and to categorise them into those that must be responded to, those that must be acknowledged and those that can be dealt with later, filed or ignored. I want you to avoid sending the messages that fall into the last category because those messages are not being received.

It is a mistake to think that everyone wants to know everything about your change initiative. In fact most people want to know very little if they feel that they will get decision data in a timely manner. The key to effective communication is to get the right message to the right person at the right time and in the right way to provoke the right outcome.

In a world of emails, text, messenger, telephones, town halls, open office environments, fly bys, etcetera it's important that the change team reduces the amount of communication. I mean reduce it to the essential. Cutting out unnecessary communications means that the messages are less likely to be mistakenly taken for routine when they require action. Because of the volume of communication we all make decisions about how we filter, otherwise we would get little else done.

In this chapter you will read about tools to segment and schedule stakeholder engagement. The outcome is to have a stakeholder bar chart that works in a very similar way to a schedule baseline, it enables the change team to plan for and engage with stakeholders whose interest and power is on the rise and therefore have a current stake and are ready, willing and able to communicate.

The Power / Interest matrix.

The PI matrix illustrates the interest and power of stakeholders and groups, relative to the project aims and objectives.

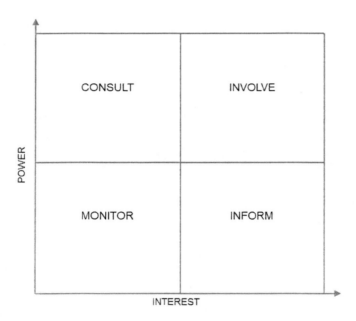

Fig. 8. Power / Interest matrix.

This well-used model illustrates the general approach that the change leader would take to manage a stakeholder in any of the four quadrants.

Monitor - Low Power, Low Interest

Typical Audience -   The user community at definition stage. Unaware.

Expectation -   Nothing: they have no interest (they may not even know about the project) and even if they did, they have no power.

Actions -   Regularly monitor their power and interest throughout the project life cycle to see if they are increasing, but do not communicate – they are not listening.

Inform - Low Power, High Interest

Typical Audience -   Suppliers bidding for tender, team members at definition stage, users at execution.

Expectation -   Knowledge: to know the detail of the drivers, objectives and plan.

Actions -   Provide access to detailed information. They want and may need to know more.

Consult - High Power, Low Interest

Typical Audience -   The sponsor at the execution stage.

Expectation -   To be involved if needed, otherwise to be kept informed.

Actions -   Consult over key decisions and provide high-level progress information.

Involve - High Power, High Interest

Typical Audience -   The client at definition and handover stages.

Expectation -   To be involved and to influence the project's management.

Actions -   Provide opportunities to make decisions.

One of the most common misinterpretations of this model lies in the use of powerful words for strategic action: **inform**, **consult** and **involve**. Particularly with *involve*, there is the perception that involving all of the stakeholders all of the time will promote a shared understanding and project harmony. In reality a majority of stakeholders are busy and don't want anything other than high-level updates and there is a minority who wield high power and are highly interested resulting in them wanting to get involved in the project.

Case Study 15: A Demanding Customer

> Steven was a project manager for an established European data communications provider. He would typically work on eight or nine projects at any one time. At one of my workshops he was telling us about one demanding customer.
>
> *"This customer had all the power, which is normal,"* Steven explained, *"but he was also quite nervous and wanted regular reassurance from me that we were on track."*
>
> *"He insisted on a two-hour meeting every Friday morning to go over the project plan in detail and update him on progress,"* lamented Steven. *"Bearing in mind that often the progress would be technically negligible I would normally manage this need through a RAG (Red, Amber, Green - traffic lights) report and perhaps a courtesy call. To manage this customer's expectations it took over one morning a week and that was for just one of my nine customers."*

Understanding power and interest.

In the context of the power / interest matrix, interest is defined as high and low. In reality there is much more granularity. For example, in some circumstances there may be a stakeholder, like the end user who, at the beginning of the project would not even know that the project was being initiated. There might also be a resource owner that knows the project is being initiated and that, if approved, will require effort. However for the resource owner this is uncertain and anyway, right now there are more pressing things on their to do list.

So for the purpose of clarity, I advise that high interest describes a sense that for the stakeholder this project represents a significant part of their daily attention. Low interest describes a sense that the project may be important (in the case of the sponsor) but it is not the most important thing in the mind of that stakeholder at that time.

Identifying power is not a simple matter of those individuals or groups with organisational or budgetary authority. There are different types of power to consider:

o Organisational: power through hierarchical position.

o Inferred or network: power through a network with powerful individuals or groups.

o Bureaucratic: power through a knowledge of processes or systems.

For the purpose of this model I recommend high power is defined as the ability to positively or negatively influence the outcome of the change initiative.

The stakeholder bar chart

The power / interest matrix has limitations, it illustrates positions of power and interest at one point in time. In reality the power and interest of individuals rise and fall at different times in the project.

The resource manager's power and interest will be at its greatest during the execution of the project phase when their resources are actually being utilised. A delay here could cause critical path slippage. However, before and after this point the ability of this stakeholder to positively or negatively influence the outcome is reduced.

The sponsor will generally wield high power throughout the life cycle but their interest will most often be technically low as they are dealing with day to day issues. Of course at decision points, and when things go well or badly their interest will be high.

The end user community will have the ability to accept or reject the solution (high power) at testing and handover stages but their interest (and anxiety) might also be high.

In Table 6, I present a variation on the power / interest matrix that reflects the changing dynamic of power and interest over the life cycle of the project, I call this a stakeholder chart.

Stakeholder	Discovery	Plan	Sign-off	Execute	Handover	Close
Steering Committee	CON	INF	INV	CON	INV	CON
Owner	INV	INV	INF	INF	INV	MON
Project Support	MON	INF	INV	CON	MON	MON
Business as Usual Management	INF	INF	CON	INF	INV	MON
User Community	MON	MON	MON	INF	INV	INV

Table 6. The stakeholder chart.

MON – Monitor (low power and interest)

INF – Inform (high interest, low power)

CON – Consult (high power, low interest)

INV – Involve (high power and interest)

On the following page, Figure 9, displays the information in a graphical way.

88

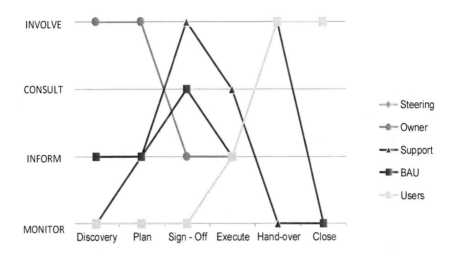

Fig. 9. Power / Interest Chart

I remember a workshop where an individual approached me at the beginning and informed me that he did not want to be with us but had been told that as part of his development plan he needed to attend. He would, he informed me, be in and out with calls and meetings but that he would make every effort not to interrupt the flow of the workshop. He was true to his word, in and out but when he was in he was very supportive and contributed a lot of his positive experiences. At the conclusion of the two days he approached me and thanked me for the course. He had found it surprisingly refreshing and a good use of time, specifically the stakeholder 'stuff' that he felt would be of use to his relationship management team.

A few weeks later when back in the same building this individual came down at break time and showed me what his team had developed off the back of the stakeholder chart, it looked very similar to Figure 14, tracking interactions with stakeholders across a prospect to sales life cycle.

Whether your preference is for the table or the chart the projected information provides the change leader with a powerful tool for anticipating and then managing the needs and expectations of stakeholders in a timely manner.

If I know what actions are approaching then I can take action in advance to attend to issues. It would be unlikely for me as a change leader to wait until the Monday morning to discuss with the task owner a task due to start that very same day. Yet it is often the case that stakeholders have been over-communicated with and are therefore tuned out of our communications or that they are engaged only at the time when their power and interest is at its peak. This means that there is no reserve of trust, understanding, rapport or relationship to call upon.

Referring briefly to the model described in Figure 9, if I select the users as a stakeholder group then I can see that, while their interest is high during execution, it is during handover and close that their power, and therefore their ability to positively or negatively influence the outcome is greatest. It would be my recommendation therefore to start engaging with the user community at the execution stage.

In another example, selecting the support function, we can see power and interest peaking at the sign-off stage. Assuming that they have at the planning stage been asked to assign resources then it would follow that at the point of sign-off their influencing ability would be greatest. A smooth and timely sign-off could be achieved through early expectation management.

Of course it is not always the case that stakeholders are willing counterparts to change initiatives. For a variety of reasons stakeholders may take up positions against the best interests of the project's objectives.

Case Study 16: Pre-Syndication.

> Marc had responsibility for the day to day running of the order management department at a medium-scale data communications provider. Marc reported in to the executive committee (ExCo) on a monthly basis and provided some insight into pre-syndication of stakeholders.

"From experience I learned that on the ExCo there were two individuals who would influence decisions the most," **Marc described.** *"It wasn't that they were the most senior just that one was very vocal and the other very considered."*

Marc went on to describe a typical ExCo meeting. *"Committee member one has very little tolerance for the detail, instead preferring the big picture strategy. If I went into too much detail I could see this person visibly switching off. I knew that it would be a struggle to get them back on board after that. However,"* **Marc continued,** *"there was this other ExCo member, committee member two who was completely the opposite. He wanted the detail and was not prepared to make a decision without it. To be honest it made the whole process of obtaining support for initiative quite challenging."*

I asked Marc how long this had gone on for and what he had done to resolve it. He told me that it had continued for several months and then went on to describe his successful strategy for achieving a successful outcome.

"I realised that I had to manage these people separately and somehow give them both what they wanted. So I started meeting with committee member two in advance of the ExCo meeting. I was very clear that I was not looking for any additional support but that I was seeking to satisfy his expectations in terms of detail in advance of the meeting. After that things went much more smoothly."

Marc explained that he did not win all of his arguments but that he probably saved four hours every month, time that he would have otherwise have spent trying to forward fix.

Successful stakeholder management does not end with the stakeholder chart, but it can be started there. By identifying in advance risks and opportunities, the change team has more time to formulate strategies to maximise or minimise exposure to these positive or negative events.

The next section identifies the stakeholder's position relative to the project's objectives and prescribes some general management strategies.

Practical Application.

If you have ever done an activity sequencing exercise with post-it notes or drawing on a white board, you will recognise the concept of scheduling stakeholder engagement and activities. Alternatively the concept is also similar to a responsibility accountability matrix (RAM) or Responsible, Accountable, Consult, Inform chart.

Map out the project life cycle in sufficient detail to be able to plot individual stakeholder moments. These moments are categorised according to when a stakeholder has the power and interest to influence the project. It's useful to put in a column or step for each sign-off milestone or gate as the stakeholders involved in this activity will be different to those involved in getting the project to that point.

Consider, seek out, ask peers and plot those stakeholders who feature during these stages, noting the relative power and interest (on a scale of 1 to 4 or perhaps MON, INF, CON, INV) during those stakeholder moments.

Conclusion

The ability to predict the points in a change life cycle when stakeholders are most able to positively or negatively influence the outcome of a change initiative is hugely beneficial. In the same way as we use a bar chart or critical path to look forwards and focus on potential points of failure, we are able to engage with and manage stakeholder expectations, hopefully removing the obstacles to support.

Of course this is not where the effort ends because we now need to start thinking about what we are going to do, what actions we are going to take to engage with and manage expectations. We will explore this in the next three chapters.

Lesson Seven:
Clear the path.

Chapter Nine: For or Against?

In the previous chapters you will have read about establishing where the role, contribution, dynamics, power and interests of your stakeholder groups have been identified. If you have applied the tools and approaches then you may also have some evidence to suggest where these stakeholders are positioned relevant to your initiative objectives.

- o Some stakeholders will be very enthusiastic about your change initiative (champions).

- o Some may seem enthusiastic while coveting your resources (politicians).

- o Some may be hostile (opponents).

Aligning objectives is an age-old tactic in management practice. Simply put if I can get everyone pulling in the same direction then I am going to find progress very straightforward.

To reiterate a point that I made in chapter eight, the early identification of potential issues gives me time to address them. This objective is a central point in the next model, the stakeholder positioning chart. It relies upon a fundamental set of process steps.

State a clear objective;

e.g. "the communications deliverables will be accepted by the end of this year"

1. Identify the stakeholders involved with achieving this objective

    o Line manager

    o Co-workers

    o Clients

    o Other senior change analysts

    o Influencers

2. With an 'X', map the ideal positions of these stakeholders against a grid of positions: *Against, Neutral,* For (*Help*) and *Make* (as in, 'Make it happen' through being an authority that can enforce the change through escalation).
3. With an 'O', map the current position of these stakeholders on the same table.
4. Identify where action must be taken to move stakeholders from current to desired positions or where action must be taken to maintain stakeholders in the desired position.

Table 7, the stakeholder positioning chart gives clues about where the time of the change team must be directed in order to align expectations.

Stakeholders	Against	Neutral	Help	Make
Line Manager		O		X
Co-Workers		OX		
Clients			OX	
Other SCA's		O	X	
Influencers		O	X	

Table 7. Stakeholder positioning chart

What the model illustrates are the gaps between the current and desired positions. The greater the gap the more effort that is required to move.

Gap analysis

What happens next is a classic gap analysis. I propose that there are only three reasons why stakeholders are not doing what they should be doing in a change initiative.

1. Unaware – they are not aware of the role that they should be playing.

2. Unable – they do not have the ability, the resource or the budget to perform the desired action.

3. Unwilling – they do not want to perform the desired action.

The responses to these positions are expressed below.

Gap	Strategy	Practical Actions
Unaware	Inform, educate	Communication, influencing, engagement
Unable	Enable	Empower, support, direct, training
Unwilling	Motivate or remove	Motivational actions, negotiation, persuasion and influencing

Table 8. Gap analysis

Case Study 17: Ready to Pull?

Andrew was a senior change manager in a financial services organisation. He explained to me how a lack of awareness at a senior level had caused problems for change managers and how it had been overcome.

"We are a structured organisation," **Andrew** started, *"we enjoy a great deal of governance from work reception through to delivery. There are decision-making boards and they generally contribute positively in keeping the change initiatives on track, delivering value."* **Andrew** went on to then describe the situation with sponsorship. *"In a lot of cases a*

sponsor would be assigned, in some cases a sponsor would volunteer, but in most cases the sponsors had a very different view of their role in a successful change initiative."

Andrew described a disconnect where change managers needed active support and participation from the sponsor, specifically around the area of championing and stakeholder management whereas the sponsor saw their role as a figurehead. The sponsors typically saw themselves as prominent at the start and at the end but that in the middle it was the role of the change manager to deliver the outcomes.

I asked Andrew what kind of issues that this caused.

"There's only so much that can be achieved through persuasion, influencing and negotiation at our level. After that it requires intervention by an individual or body that has authority – authority to influence or ultimately to make things happen. We had the governance boards but they were inflexible, meeting only once a fortnight or month. In a nutshell, this caused delays," Andrew explained. *"We had to delay actions until the change boards could be used to wield authority."*

I went on to ask Andrew what he felt was needed.

"What we needed were sponsors who understood the need for support. For them to be actively involved, asking questions, challenging and ultimately ready, willing and able to intervene on behalf of the change management team," Andrew said.

In 2008 a framework for change was implemented across the business. From a sponsorship perspective it had one significant addition, it prescribed the role and responsibilities of the change sponsor. Where previously there had been role descriptions only for the management team, this initiative provided a starting point. I asked Andrew to tell me about the impact of this change.

"Initially it was just a page on the intranet site but it was something to bring to the change board when change teams and sponsors were being assigned. The effect of that was that, to start with, sponsors were less inclined to volunteer and there was some resistance. However, one of the points that was clarified in this document was ownership. From that point forward it was clearly documented that the sponsor was accountable for delivery. Prior to that it was assumed that the change manager owned the change," Andrew told me. *"The change managers became better at managing the expectations of the sponsors. The sponsors, newly*

enfranchised by this accountability, were generally delighted to understand how little the change managers actually needed from them. Consequently they were generally very happy to provide support when required."

Of the three gaps, evidence shows that a lack of awareness is the most common. The reasons for this vary but can often be a lack of communication or a lack of engagement. Change managers, uncomfortable influencing and persuading upwards, may shirk from challenging sponsors.

It may be the case that as we start to address gaps we move a stakeholder from being unaware to unable, or we enable them only for them to become unwilling. I stated that one of the strategies is to remove those that are unwilling to help. This is essential. If we are to complete the scope of the initiative then the contributors must be willing to perform to the required standard. If this is not the case and the stakeholder cannot be removed then the scope of the change initiative must be redefined.

The strategies for managing stakeholders' expectations are not limited to those described in this section and will be explored more fully in the next.

Practically speaking

I've mentioned earlier that I use an excel spreadsheet to gather lots of stakeholder data together in one place as a kind of stakeholder dictionary.

Understanding the position of stakeholders relevant to your change will prove to be an ongoing process. It might be that the first estimate of a stakeholder's position was incorrect, or that events have conspired to move them.

This investment in consistently checking back will result in both the maintenance of support and an early warning system to enable the change team to respond before there are schedule-impacting issues.

www.ajpconsulting.org

Conclusion

Stakeholders' positions relevant to the objectives of the change initiative will be based upon many factors: their experience of previous initiatives; their alignment with the outcomes; their contribution; how they stand to gain or suffer from the result.

The change leader needs to discover not only the position of stakeholders but the reasons for the disconnect and must take action to move or maintain until alignment is achieved. This process is ongoing and is very much likened to the tour guide or group leader who is charged with constantly checking to ensure that everyone is together, present and accounted for.

Lesson Eight:

All stakeholders present and accounted for.

Chapter Ten: Steer the Course

In chapter eight you read about the stakeholder chart and in chapter nine about stakeholder positioning. I said that this process of stakeholder categorisation is not the end of stakeholder management, though it may be the beginning. In this chapter you will read about practical actions to employ in order to maintain and move stakeholders to gain and retain the guiding coalition of support.

The way in which we manage stakeholders will always be influenced by a variety of factors:

o   The culture of the organisation.

o   The preferences of the individual.

o   The aims and objectives of the individual.

o   Their position relevant to the change.

o   The constraints around the initiative.

Case Study 18: A Journey

Mike is the CEO of a startup technology company. Six months after starting the company he has three clients and two employees. His company delivers business-processing improvements. Mike has a vision for his company; he sees it as the largest outsourcing company in the world. This is Mike's project.

In the beginning Mike has a limited amount of stakeholders: the bank manager, his staff, the client organisations and his client contacts. Mike's strategy is to manage these stakeholders as three groups.

- o The bank: Mike takes a respectful collaborative approach when he consults with the bank manager; keeping him informed and on side with positive messages about growth while tactfully asking for advice and guidance on business development challenges. The aim is to keep the bank contented and supporting.

- o The staff: Mike likes to be in control and does not yet see the need to consult with his staff. The team is a small one and Mike is very attentive in terms of recognition and reward so morale is very positive. The aim is for the team to execute Mike's vision quickly and effectively.

- o The clients: As a startup company, Mike believes that his clients like responsiveness and adaptability so he collaborates heavily. Mike recognises that this is time-consuming but critical to building the relationships and the products that will make the company the world's foremost business process outsource provider. The aim is to demonstrate that the company listens and responds quickly and effectively.

Twelve months later and the company is growing fast. Mike has secured some venture capital funding with which to expand into new premises. There are now one hundred members of staff, including a senior management team of three (finance, operations, business development) and ten supervisory management staff. Mike's company has just secured its first multinational client and in total now services the business processing needs of thirty client organisations.

The number of stakeholders has grown and Mike's stakeholder strategy has become correspondingly more complex.

- o VC Organisation: Mike no longer has to deal with the bank. The VC firm are primarily interested in the financial performance of the organisation. Mike's relationship with the VC firm is much more hands-off than with the bank.

Mike keeps the VC firm informed; the aim is to minimise the involvement of the VC firm while maintaining support.

o The management team: Mike still likes to be in control and largely dictates strategy to the team. The company is growing quickly so it's hard to argue with Mike's business strategy and besides, the management team are well-rewarded and recognised by Mike so morale is good. The aim is that the executive management team translates and delivers Mike's vision throughout the company.

o The supervisory management team: Mike likes to walk around the company and talk to the supervisors and staff but neither consults nor collaborates with the staff. Morale is high as the staff like Mike and they like to be part of the success story. The aim is to reassure the staff that Mike is still around and that he cares.

o The clients: There are now two tiers of client, the complex and large and the small and straightforward. Mike's approach to the former is collaborative as before but with the latter the company is less flexible but still listens. The aim is to maintain the flexible and adaptable offering but also to reduce the volume of customisation and deliver a consistent and reliable product.

Two years after starting and the company has just floated on the Alternative Investment Market. A new office has been opened in Frankfurt with projects to open in Paris, Milan and Madrid in the pipeline. The company is an unmitigated success and the flotation demonstrated this with the issue being heavily over-subscribed. With so much change and growth in such a short period of time Mike's stakeholder strategy is now becoming honed and well-developed.

o Shareholders: Mike no longer has to deal with the VC firm but instead has to report to shareholders. Mike's interactions with shareholders are few but important so he prepares well and delivers positive statements and interviews at key points, not limited to the AGM. He describes performance and future plans. His goal is to maintain interest, support and growth.

- o The executive leadership team: The original management team has been promoted to more senior positions and now provide leadership to the line management structure below them. Mike consults more with the leadership team now. He still maintains a dictatorial approach but is more prepared to listen, specifically to feedback as he is much more removed from the day to day operations of the company. Mike expects his leadership team to demonstrate and execute a robust approach to stakeholder management. Mike's aim is that the leadership team translate his direction to the operational and delivery teams, maintaining morale and growth.

- o Supervisors and staff: It is the responsibility of the leadership team to manage these stakeholders. The business has grown and so has both the complexity of the communication channels and the need for reliable processes. The aim is to collaborate with the operational and delivery teams to ensure that process, performance and morale grow together.

- o The clients: Mike now focuses on the high-end, complex and large scale clients. His approach is to be no less flexible but less collaborative, at least in the negotiating phase. The high-end clients want more predictability and reliability than flair and ingenuity. The aim is to build stable, long-term relationships.

In summary, Mike's stakeholder management journey has demonstrated adaptability and flexibility. He has sought to anticipate his stakeholders' needs and to align them with his business aims and objectives. This strategy has earned reward and the company continues to grow.

Practical management strategies

The Project Management Institute (PMI) recognises a stakeholder management strategy as "a plan to increase the support for and reduce the obstacles and resistance for a project". The following list describes some generic approaches and when they should be employed:

- **Top down (dictatorial):** Considered essential when compliance is mandatory. Like a change in legislation or where the cost of non-compliance is high. This approach would see the sponsor and the change team dictating behaviours and performance.

- **Bottom up (consultative):** Considered essential when the initiative relies upon a broad base of support and acceptance, like culture change. This approach would see the change team involved in promoting the benefits, employing champions and building consensus.

- **Middle ground (collaborative):** Considered as the preferred approach when there is the risk of rejection or negative impact from the recipients of and the contributors to the change. This approach would see the sponsor and senior stakeholders articulating the need for compliance as well as illustrating the benefits to the other stakeholders.

	Speed to Implement	Authority Required	Motivational Impact
Dictatorial	High	High to Absolute	Negative
Consultative	Low	Low	Positive
Collaborative	Medium	Medium	Positive

Table 9. Management Strategies

These approaches are generic because in practice the application of stakeholder strategy is fluid. In the same way as Mike listened to his stakeholders and altered his strategy, so the change leader is constantly adapting and improving the strategy in order to achieve the aims.

Practical communication

A key aspect of stakeholder management is communication, and specifically the sending and receiving of decision information that will influence the strategy.

In a typical 'Plan - Do - Review' cycle the strategy is constantly updated to reflect the effectiveness of the actions and the wants and needs of the stakeholders. Throughout stakeholder management the leaders should be asking two questions:

1. Can I still achieve my objectives?

2. Do we still need the outcome?

If the answer to these questions remains yes then we can look at the communications aspect in a little more detail. Specifically at a sender - receiver model.

The sender-receiver model works in the same way as the Plan - Do - Review cycle except that it is more sophisticated in terms of the information that is being reviewed.

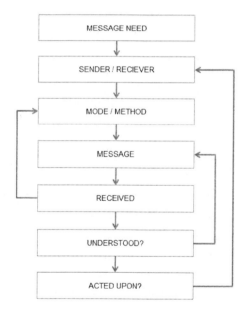

Fig. 10. Sender-Receiver model

The stakeholder strategy relies upon the achievement of specific objectives, in the model above this is referred to as the Action.

104

Examples of this action could be:

- ○ Informing colleagues of the benefits of the change.

- ○ Releasing resources at the time and volume agreed.

- ○ Maintaining vocal support in the executive stakeholder review.

To illustrate this further, imagine a situation where you need to overcome some resistance in the leadership team of the organisation. This resistance is manifest in resources that had previously been promised being withheld. As the change leader you do not have the opportunity to speak to the leadership team, even if they know who you are. So you execute a communication strategy to obtain the required resources (I refer to this situation as not having a licence. Access to individuals is based upon having a licence to approach).

1. Identify a member of the leadership team that has influence, is positive (a champion, perhaps) and that can be relied upon to communicate a message (this person has the licence).

2. Construct a message that demonstrates the business benefits of the change in a way that will appeal to a majority of the leadership board and overcome the resistance.

3. Provide the message and any supporting information to the messenger (the leadership team member).

4. Check with the messenger to ensure that the message was delivered.

5. Seek validation that the message was presented in a compelling way and that it was understood.

6. Seek validation that the message was acted upon and that the resources have now been released.

If the answer to any of steps 4, 5 or 6 is in the negative then the stakeholder manager must go back and either change the wording of the message or the delivery method. The table on the following page offers a useful guide.

Stakeholder	Stake	Contribution	Current Position	Desired Position	Actions	Delivery
Sponsor	Strategy	Authority	Help	Make	Maintain support with regular, short updates.	PM
Line Manager	Reputation	Resources	Neutral	Help	Show the benefits. Show the minimum disruption to their BAU[4].	Sponsor
End User	Easier life	Acceptance	Against	Help	Sell the benefits.	Champion

Table 10. A stakeholder strategy document.

Conclusion

In this chapter you have read about stakeholder positioning, the reasons why stakeholders are not doing what we want them to do, and some strategies and actions to position them positively to gain and maintain a guiding coalition of stakeholders.

The conclusion is that while identification, understanding and modelling helps greatly in achieving the goal of stakeholder support, they all constitute the start of what is a long process.

The skipper of a sailing vessel will tell you that 'reaching' (sailing with the wind mainly behind you) is far more comfortable than going into the wind and becoming 'close hauled' but that sometimes the voyage

---

[4] Business As Usual

requires the latter. Stakeholder management is very much like steering a sailboat; paying attention to all of the inputs from sail, tiller and crew and sometimes steering into the wind to make the best course.

Lesson Nine:

Steer into the wind.

Chapter Eleven: Overcome Cultural Obstacles

The monkey enters the cage for the first time and greedily eyes the bunch of bananas placed at the top of a short ladder, barely a leap away. The other three monkeys do not seem to have noticed the bananas but they have noticed the monkey, our newcomer. The monkey does not know why the others are looking at him nor does he know why the bananas are untouched and so driven by a thousand years of genetic heritage he climbs the ladder to get to the food. Before he gets three rungs up the short ladder the first object hits him, quickly followed by others. In shock the monkey realises that it is his peers, the other monkeys, that are pelting him. He retreats to find cover and as soon as he retreats off the first rung of the ladder the pelting stops.

This urban myth[5] describes how the resident monkeys had been trained not to climb the ladder by first being sprayed with water when they climbed the ladder and then latterly by being sprayed with water when one of the other monkeys climbed the ladder. This story describes the beginning of a social norm, or cultural norm. Another way of describing

---

[5] It seems unlikely that this story is founded on any behavioural or scientific evidence or process but nevertheless proves an interesting and popular anecdote.

culture is 'the way it's done around here.' It is often the case that the origins of the cultural norm have been forgotten or lost but nevertheless, unchallenged the cultural norms continue, and they are strong.

This chapter builds on the lessons of the previous five that were focused on creating strategies to manage and build relationships with stakeholders. It's very often the case that cultures are in place that make the implementation and embedding of change difficult to achieve. Endeavouring to understand these cultures and the challenges that they pose will provide the change team with more time in which to formulate strategies to maximise opportunities and minimise risks.

Case Study 19: No Air Raids Today

> When I was researching an article about to-do lists I came across a piece written on the web site of R. Todd Stevens PhD[6]. In it the author describes how a quality consultant, visiting a medium-sized, family manufacturing firm, spotted an anomaly on a daily report. The report was completed on a paper form that itself was a photocopy that had degraded in quality to the point that many of the headings were ineligible. What caught his eye was that amongst the daily reporting information collected on this form, there was a box that had a zero reported in it. In fact it had had a zero reported in it for the past year. The consultant was unable to read the description for the box, such was the degradation of type quality through photocopying.

> When the consultant asked the employees what the zero was for they admitted that they did not know. Only that there had been a zero in that box for as long as anyone could remember. Eventually the consultant found the master copies and the longer version of the faded report he found and deciphered the key to the box, a description which read, 'N⁰· Air Raids Today.'

It's amazing how much of what we do is based upon accepted cultural norms.

---

[6] http://www.rtodd.com/notebook/2010/no-air-raids-today.aspx

Case Study 20: One to Five

> A colleague of mine, Jill, came back from a global conference and described to me how the facilitator for that day had asked them to complete an exercise. They each had to hold up their hands and count to five, using their fingers, simultaneously. Apparently each person did this slightly different. Some people started with a closed hand and opened, from the thumb one to five. Others had a similar approach but started with the littlest finger. Some of the delegates started with an open hand and closed fingers and then thumb, while others used a second hand to tick off the fingers and thumb.

Of course the point is not just that we have cultural differences, the delegates did happen to come from a variety of cultural and national backgrounds, but that we have preferences. The interesting part, like in the previous story, is when you ask people to tell you why they do things in a certain way. No one could tell exactly why they counted to five in this particular way.

o   Their parents?

o   Their education and schooling?

In a business change environment, culture can present barriers:

o   The recipients of the change are used to working in a particular way.

o   The resources are used to contributing in a specific way.

o   Change management is given little respect within the organisation.

o   User acceptance testing is always compromised to meet time and cost budgets.

These are a few examples of the kind of cultural obstacles that the change leader must identify, accept and/or overcome in order to deliver successful and lasting change. To achieve the necessary change integration requires an understanding of the sub-cultures within the delivery and recipient organisations so that effective processes for collaboration and communication can be effectively implemented.

Case Study 21: An Amusing Revolution.

This story happened in a fast-growing technology organisation.

The first-line technical support call centre was not a fun place to work. The first thing that you noticed upon entering was the buzz of conversation, the second thing that you noticed was the call information board on the wall with large red LED statistics on calls answered, calls waiting and the percentage of calls dropped. Individuals, all wearing a shirt and tie with headsets on, were navigating between two 22-inch monitors displaying call logging and network operational statistics. The first-line technical support call centre was an environment where measurement was king and performance was in the statistics.

A typical caller issue would be an outage. A failure in the comms link that a part of the client organisation relied upon. The job that first-line technical support had was initially to gather details of when, how long, location, specifics and contact details and then to either identify an existing outage and tag or to log a new fault for technical investigation by a network or field engineer.

Bruce was just another call centre executive who had demonstrated the ability to take on board quickly the technical nature of enquiries and to respond knowledgeably and calmly to demanding and often irate callers with technical issues.

Bruce didn't set out to change the culture. In fact it's likely that he would not be able to describe culture change to you, however, Bruce changed things because he had a view of how things could be in the call centre and his view was different from the existing one.

If you visited the call centre six months after Bruce started you would notice the same buzz of conversation and you would notice the call information board but what you would also notice would be the occasional outbreak of laughter, a bright mix of colourful tee shirts and tops, and movement; people moving around.

This is a call centre environment where measurement was critical and statistics described performance but it was also an environment where customer satisfaction was driven as much by the speed of problem resolution as it was by demonstrating empathy with a genuine smile.

As you observed more you would start to see the interaction between the call centre executives. There would be exchanges verbally and on instant messenger, occasionally executives would leave their desk to chat to a friend. Talk would be of lunch venues, the next team night out and what the latest amusing stories were.

If you asked the team members to describe their team you would hear something like:

o   We are a tight-knit team.

o   We work hard and we party hard.

o   We are professionals.

o   We have a laugh here!

o   The boss is okay.

o   Bruce is hilarious!

It's the last comment that provides the necessary insight into this change.

Bruce came into a team where hard work was mandated and Bruce was happy to work hard but he was not happy to do it without a smile on his face. Without meaning to, Bruce started influencing those around him. In the first instance it would be the random person with whom he was sharing a desk that day. Bruce would tell a joke, point out something funny or describe an entertaining night out all the while answering customer calls with speed, accuracy and a smile.

Bruce started the lunch outings. Before Bruce everyone had a sandwich at their desk, or made something in the kitchen before bringing it back to their desk. Bruce went to a local pub. In the beginning it was just Bruce plus whoever else was on lunch break. Later other groups went out when Bruce was not on a break.

Bruce organised the first team night out. At first it was two colleagues but the next day, when the funny stories emerged, others realised that they could have fun too. Nowadays everyone organises nights out, it's the fun thing to do.

Bruce was the first person to come in without a tie and the first person to wear a tee shirt (at first it was underneath his shirt, with a couple of buttons undone). Graham, the manager, initially had an issue with the shirt and tie thing; after all, Graham had always worn a shirt and tie. However, Graham was smart enough to notice that Bruce was a high performer and that he was positively influencing the performance and attitude of others in the team.

Bruce is not a revolutionary. Bruce is not interested in upsetting or changing things, he just wants to be himself and has a clear image of the way things should be. The thing is, others want to do what Bruce does, they want to be with him, laughing, having fun, working and playing hard.

Bruce is a founder, an individual who can influence and change culture. Surprisingly, Bruce does it from the bottom up, he does so without organisational authority.

Analysis

How was it that Bruce managed to change the culture of this team so quickly, radically and totally? I will argue that in order for there to be culture change there needs to be a number of elements in attendance.

1. Culture – an existing cultural norm (or base) from which to depart from.

2. Resources – the resources required to communicate the benefits and then provide the new facility.

3. Motivation – a desire to change.

4. Politics – the right degree of support or acquiescence.

There was a very formal culture in place, and everyone conformed to it.

Bruce, a good personality and a tee shirt didn't require much in the way of resources. He had instant messenger and he had the local public house.

The vision of where Bruce wanted the team dynamic to go was so much more bright and compelling than the existing one that motivation was never really a problem however, it could have been had it not been for the actions of Graham, the manager.

Graham had a clear vision of what a call centre should be, and in his way he had been the first founder of the call centre culture. However he was insightful enough to realise that the team's performance could be enhanced in ways other than those with which he was familiar.

Graham did not facilitate this culture change by openly supporting it but he did nothing to stop it as long as performance was maintained.

In the following pages you will read about some practical ways to overcome cultural obstacles:

o   Engage with influencers.

o   Develop catalysts.

o   Follow a path.

Engage the key influencers

In his book, Organisational Culture and Leadership[7] Edgar H. Schein talks about founders. Founders are the individuals who found cultures and are often prominent at the beginning of an organisation or a movement. Founders usually have a strong view of how teams should operate and perform and these views are translated into actions and then norms.

When I describe key influencers I am talking about founders new and old. The founders of existing culture and the founders of new culture.

In this example Bruce was the founder and the influencer of the change. That he is unaware of the impact of his actions is irrelevant at this stage. The important fact is that we have identified Bruce as the individual who can facilitate change.

As a change leader we are on the lookout for these influencers. Sometimes we refer to them as champions but I believe that champions are more like cheerleaders than the powerful force for change that I relate to the influencer. Once we have identified the influencers the change leader must describe a role for this individual, the role that they will perform to facilitate the desire change. The second step is to get that individual to perform the role as described.

---

[7] Wiley, 1992 – 2nd Edition.

I will refer back to the previous section on stakeholder management here and specifically to the gap analysis section. The following questions would be pertinent:

- o What is the position of the influencer relevant to the objectives of the change initiative?

- o Can they be re-positioned into the 'Make' column?

- o What is the reason for any disconnect between what we want them to be doing and what they are doing?

- o Do they agree with the outcome or can they be persuaded of its importance?

- o What actions do the change team need to take to gain and maintain the commitment and support of this key influencer?

- o If support cannot be gained or if the influencer is likely to position themselves against the objectives of the change then what will or can the change team do?

I will illustrate a planned approach using a flow diagram in Figure 11 on the following page. The objective is to achieve a successful outcome through engagement with others to overcome cultural obstacles.

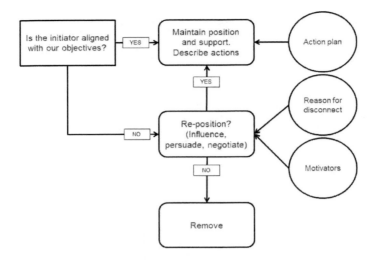

Fig. 11. Engaging with influencers.

The flow diagram in Figure 11 represents the logical flow of actions and inputs.

1. The objective of the engagement is to establish positive support from the influencer and the first step is to establish whether the influencer is aligned with the change objectives and therefore likely to respond in a predictable way.

2. If so then the change team should monitor this situation and take actions to ensure that they remain supportive while establishing a situation where the influencer will act in accordance with the prescribed plan[8].

---

[8] Note that an initiator or influencer that is aligned and also enfranchising their explicit support may be two separate things and require a high degree of flexibility, collaboration and patience from the change leader.

3. If there is a disconnect then the change team must look at ways of bridging the gap. Two key inputs here will be the reason for the disconnect (unaware, unwilling, unable) and insights into the levers that will motivate the influencer to change their position.

4. If this re-positioning is successful then refer to point 2. If there is no possible way that the influencer's influence can be either harnessed or nullified then they must be removed in order for the change to be successful.

Point 4 seems harsh and final and I receive a lot of discussion around this point.

o It is not always possible to remove a person.

o What if they contribute positively in every other way?

o I cannot remove this person as they are senior in the organisation.

My response is to acknowledge these points with empathy. It is a very final step, however consider the outcomes if a change influencer remains in opposition to the desired change? The effort required to overcome such resistance is not insurmountable but it is difficult, and time- and resource-consuming. So the change team, in a situation where the influencer remains contrary to the objectives must ask the following questions:

o Is the change necessary?

o Are there alternatives that the influencer will support?

o Can the influencer be sidelined or their effect nullified?

I would then refer back to the four points described in the analysis of the last case study:

o Culture - Is the culture established?

o Resources - Are there sufficient resources to overcome this resistance?

o Motivation - Are the individuals in the team motivated to change (despite the preferences of the change influencer)?

- o Politics - Can the right degree of support or acquiescence be established without or against the influencer?

- o Essentially the question that the change leader will come back to will be: Do the benefits of this change merit the actions and effort that will be required to facilitate it?

If the answer to the question is yes and if the stakeholders agree with this answer then the action to remove / replace the influencer will be the only one.

Summary

Engaging with the key influencers is part of the wider stakeholder management strategy and actions. However, it is a discrete and essential part of overcoming cultural obstacles.

Building on the previous insights into stakeholder management, a positive strategy can be made effective or not by the person being used to deliver the message and influencers are perfectly positioned if the change team can enfranchise them.

Develop the catalysts.

Sometimes, regardless of influencers, an organisation or part of the organisation is ready for change and welcomes it.

In an earlier chapter I told the story of a business processing outsourcing company that had experienced rapid growth and had been required to massively change its delivery focus to meet the wants and needs of its newer customers. You may recall that I described how the business had been successful because it had been able to flexibly and quickly respond to its customers' demands. It had developed a reputation as an innovative and dynamic supplier of cutting edge solutions. However as the scale and size of its customers had increased, it was reacting to increased demands for solutions that were robust and reliable.

The change had been a success and that in part was due to the power and leadership style of the CEO but this was not the only reason.

o   The organisation had been operating in a stable style for eight years and so had a firm base from which to move towards change.

o   The organisation was successful and possessed the financial and organisational resources to develop and deliver the necessary process and product changes.

o   The staff in the organisation were generally receptive to a change that meant more certainty around processes, responsibilities and roles.

o   There was a political will to achieve the changes. Distilled down to basics, if the organisation were unable to change it would start to decline or it would have to develop a different market strategy.

I referred to these four points earlier on in this chapter and proposed that these four factors must be in place for change to be readily deployed:

1.   Stable culture.

2.   Resources available.

3.   Motivation to change.

4.   Political will.

On the subject of change, most would agree with me that the perception of a positive future state is a powerful motivator as would be the perception that the current state is unsustainable.

If the organisation, like the one in the earlier example, is accustomed to change (entrepreneurial, evolving) then the culture or the catalysts are in place and so leveraging them to promote change is likely.

If the organisation is not accustomed to change and development then the change team must search for other catalysts to leverage, either to promote a positive future view or the perception that the current one is unsustainable.

Practically speaking

The business analyst is often referred to as a catalyst for change. It's no surprise when you consider that their function is to gain a deep and fundamental understanding of the business.

Trust is a key factor in transformation and overcoming cultural obstacles. The business analyst, the change team members or business as usual champions already have or can gain that trust through demonstrations of empathy[9], familiarity and shared experiences.

Some of the typical obstacles like mistrust, comfort in certainty, solidarity can themselves be turned into powerful catalysts.

o Demonstrate to those that have no trust that there is a shared identity, a shared journey and a shared outcome. Steve Jobs once used the idea of a shared enemy to good effect when in 1984 he suggested to the world that IBM was the enemy and that it was turning its guns on all the small innovators.

o Where there is solidarity there is a powerful union. Instead of trying to break that down consider what could be achieved if that powerful union was for you rather than against you. The key to unlocking this power tends to rest with powerful individuals.

o The sense of comfort in what is done now is based upon a fear of the future. Consider what would happen were the current status quo to be threatened and a bright future be revealed? The change then becomes salvation rather than damnation.

Summary

The dictionary states that, 'a catalyst is a substance that increases the rate of a chemical reaction without itself undergoing any permanent change.'

Catalysts can be individuals, they can be situations (like frustration or trends) that can accelerate a reaction. If the reaction can be built upon,

---

[9] See chapter twelve.

channelled, guided effectively then the change team can use it as a launch pad. Some potential launch pads include:

o   Frustration with processes, systems or environment.

o   A strong workers' culture, union or council.

o   Sympathetic and liked supervisory managers.

o   External factors such as market growth / contraction.

Follow a culture change plan

In chapter nine you read about the communication model and in particular the importance of both setting an objective and using checks to ensure that it had been received, understood and acted upon. The same philosophy applies to culture change and it starts with a question: what is the outcome and how will I know that I am on track to achieving it.

Bate (1995[10]) outlines a number of approaches to delivering culture change:

o   Aggressive.

o   Conciliative.

o   Corrosive.

o   Indoctrinative.

He goes on to describe how and when these approaches should be used.

Aggressive, this approach is often used to 'un-freeze' an organisation at the beginning of a change initiative and might involve changing roles, responsibilities and lines of reporting. The aim of the aggressive approach is to consciously disrupt the existing status quo. I have seen this used effectively in situations where there has been a historical tendency to go back to 'the old ways' once the change has been implemented. The aggressive approach means that there is nowhere to

---

[10] Bate, P. (1995) Strategies for Cultural Change, Oxford, Butterworth – Heinemann.

go back to and can be used when motivation is low. (IT projects will often have a step where the old or current solution is entirely removed so that there is no alternative but to use the new.)

Conciliative, this approach is often used where there is a need for collaboration or where buy-in at the lowest level of the organisation is required. This approach works well when the culture is not stable or after an initial aggressive approach has been employed. A conciliative approach results in the change being perceived as 'our change' and has a greater chance of sticking but attracts criticism because of the amount of time it takes.

Corrosive, this approach involves the subtler actions of manipulation, negotiation and persuasion. It is not a fast-fix approach like 'aggressive' nor is it a collaborative approach like 'conciliative'. It could be described as fix now, explain later. The term corrosive can be applied to the subtle but final approach to change and also to the potentially corrosive affect it can have on relationships. An appropriate use of the corrosive approach is where the political environment is negative and where aspects of the change may have to happen in a subtle way.

Indoctrinative, this approach seeks to normalise (re-freeze) through the application of norms and processes. For this approach to be successful requires the organisation to have been unfrozen and be ready to accept the changes.

In reality the change will require a combination of these approaches. Perhaps starting off with an aggressive approach to break the ice, followed by a period of conciliation to gain consensus and explain the benefits. In the meantime corrosive strategies could be employed to break down resistance in individuals and prepare the teams for change. Once the team and the stakeholders are receptive then an indoctrinative approach can be used to embed the norms and finally conciliative normalising of the processes to embed them.

Practically speaking

It's outside the scope of this book go into detail about carrying out culture change initiatives, other than to say have a clear objective, clarify milestones and deliverables, monitor, control and be prepared to change your plans.

Through leadership, the clear communication of a vision, engaging with and winning stakeholder support, demonstrating empathy, flexing communication and management styles the culture change plan becomes personal.

Conclusion

Cultural norms are necessary for any organisation to function and they are a prerequisite for change (they provide the solid foundation).

Understanding the drivers for change, how to identify the key influencers, how to engage with catalysts and how to apply different approaches provides the change leader with a toolkit and insights.

For change to be effectively initiated, embedded and concluded, cultural norms must be challenged, modified and then refrozen.

Change is difficult and challenging and mostly unwelcome. However, history clearly shows that it can and does happen when a visionary and inspirational leader is there to follow. Overcoming cultural obstacles is not simply about being inspirational and visionary of course, it takes a great deal of strategy and work behind the scenes but without a clear leader to follow it becomes very much more difficult.

Lesson Ten:

Stand out from the crowd.

Chapter Twelve: Inspire and Motivate the Team

Chapter eleven was all about overcoming cultural obstacles and mainly focused on the recipients of the change. In this chapter I am addressing the team responsible for delivering the change. Cultural norms and obstacles are also at play here and I will be exploring the themes of inspiring and motivating the team to perform.

Question, what is the difference between motivation and manipulation?

This was a rhetorical question posted on Twitter by a friend and colleague. The comment aroused quite a lot of interest because of the use of that word, manipulation. It strikes a lot of people as describing activities that are "below board" or underhand. I prefer the word "positioning" to manipulation but conceptually I refer to the words of Dale Carnegie, a phrase quoted earlier in this book, *there is only one way on God's earth to get someone to do something and that is to get them to want to do it.*

The change team is typically comprised of individuals contributing in a discrete way towards change objectives. In fact this description is closer to a group, the group becomes a team when their objectives become aligned. In some circumstances the change team will be wholly accountable to the change leader. In this case the team are likely to know each other and be used to working in the peculiar conditions of a change initiative. More typically however, is a situation where diverse individuals from different parts of a business or from different organisations work in a variety of ways to deliver an aspect of the project. These roles include but are not limited to:

1. Administrators.

2. Subject matter experts.

3. Decision makers.

4. Resource owners.

The challenge for the change leader is that it is desirable and sometimes crucial for these team members to work together in a close and collaborative way and for the individuals to be motivated and inspired to respond to the demanding, changing and shared objectives of the change environment.

Case Study 22: Jelly Babies

"Theirs was a unique bond which develops between the participants of great adventures. They moved easily among each other with a handshake here, a quiet word there. There were always smiles and laughter. Why not, who would not want to be part of this atmosphere?"

This is a quote from 'Global Challenge, Leadership Lessons from the World's Toughest Yacht Race[11]'.

Fourteen sturdy fifty-foot yachts lie waiting for the ultimate challenge of sailing around the world the "wrong" way, against the prevailing tides and wind. One of the interesting aspects of this race is that, like the Clipper venture series, the majority of the crew will have little to no sailing experience. They embark upon this adventure, guided by a professional skipper and mate, to find and test themselves in extremely harsh conditions.

The book tells the story of the race and gives an insight into the leadership styles and stories of the 14 skippers and their crews.

---

[11] Published in 1997 and authored by Humphrey Walters, Peter and Rosie Mackie and Andrea Bacon.

In the book there are lots of examples of inspirational leadership against a backdrop that most of us will never face but which translate directly into the setup and maintenance of project teams. The book concluded that certain high performance behaviours (HPBs) appeared to predict superior performance if used by leaders and teams faced with complex, unpredictable environments.

- Information Search
- Concept Formation
- Conceptual Flexibility
- Empathy
- Teamwork
- Developing People
- Influence
- Building Confidence
- Presentation
- Proactivity
- Continuous Improvement

One of the skippers, Mike Golding on the yacht Group Four, takes with him a large bag of Jelly Babies and describes how the little sweets became a small but significant motivating factor.

"In an ocean race there are physical challenges and there are mental challenges. The cohesion of the team is challenged by the cramped physical environment and the lack of comforts. Physically it is demanding because despite the shift roster there are times when the entire crew must come on to a tilted, heaving and water washed deck to change a foresail, or affect an emergency maneuver."

Every time that the crew encounter and overcome a significantly challenging obstacle the skipper gives each one of the crew a Jelly Baby. The important thing to note here is that this is not made into a show. On the contrary the skipper quietly ensures that each person receives a sweet, no comment is made but everyone recognises the gesture. In this small way everyone feels part of the success, no matter what their contribution was.

I admit to having used this approach on all of my subsequent projects. If you ever met a member of my project team all you would have to do to elicit a smile would be to mention the sweet box that resided in the top drawer of my desk. It's small, powerful and motivational. This gesture is inspirational because it demonstrates empathy and emphasises the sense of teamwork.

Two things have always stood out for me from the first moment that I read Global Challenge:

1. The sailing adventure is immense and I have huge respect for the skippers and crew members who participated.

2. The HPBs are hard to implement and maintain in a business as usual environment but are really relevant to the uncertain, complex and challenging nature of change and projects.

The purpose of this chapter is to look at ways in which the change leader can tap into the interests, drivers and desires of the project stakeholders and then to take the appropriate actions, apply the correct leadership approach and align objectives so that the change initiative is successful.

Actions to Consider.

1. Employing inspirational leadership.

2. Team building.

3. Demonstrating empathy.

4. Identifying and understanding the wants and needs of the team members.

5. One to one reviews and coaching.

6. Employing active listening.

Inspirational Leadership

Inspirational leaders seem to make great decisions all of the time. Inspirational leaders inspire those around them to do great things. Inspirational leaders are the leaders that we remember, the ones that created a great environment, the ones that were present and visible during times of great change or movement.

Leaders are apparent everywhere at home and at work. Inspirational leaders are those individuals who we are inspired to follow despite their position, authority and leadership. Revolutions are generally led by inspired individuals without means, portfolio or assets; see William Wallace, Muammar Gaddafi, Guiseppe Garibaldi and one Che Guevara who said this about revolutionaries. *"At the risk of seeming ridiculous, let me say this, that the true revolutionary is guided by a feeling of great love... we must strive every day so that this love of living humanity will be transformed into actual deeds, into acts that serve as examples, as a moving force."*

Case Study 23: The Listening Point.

Andy worked for a UK-based global computer systems retailer. Andy was a project manager reporting into a programme director responsible for delivering a web-based purchasing system that had the ability to allow the full spectrum of its customers to purchase computer systems simply without the need to go to a sales person. This retailer listed Fortune 500 and small to medium-sized organisations as its customers. The challenge was to deliver a solution that presented an appropriate purchasing schema to these diverse customers.

When I asked Andy to describe the culture he stated, *"Command and control, signified by silos at every level. We did not share resources and information, rather we competed for it."*

I asked Andy to describe how this culture was manifest in the team.

"We were disenfranchised, focusing on measures, and experts at producing one-page PowerPoint presentations on the status of our projects."

In 2008 the retailer brought in a new project director to take over the programme. Andy observed his behaviour on the first programme review meeting.

"Everyone came with their one page PowerPoint slides and proceeded to highlight progress in their projects. Robert listened for about 90 minutes, until all of the 40 contributors had finished and he then quietly asked, 'I've heard what you have been doing but my question is what are we going to do to get this programme back on its feet?'"

From that point forwards there was a significant shift of focus from "I" to "We". Robert introduced a cascade of objectives and he actively encouraged the views, opinions and recommendations of his project managers.

I asked Andy to describe what the observable impact of this culture change was.

"It gave people freedom; it empowered them and they started communicating. Where before there had been little collaboration now there was specific collaboration, focused on achieving the overall objectives."

"Robert was very focused on our being professional," Andy went on to explain. *"He talked a lot about the way in which we delivered having an equal, if not greater influence on the final programme than what we delivered."*

Robert also had that leadership trait of being virtually invisible when he was not needed but immediately on hand when he was. I asked Andy to describe what happened when Robert was on the scene of an issue or a problem.

"He asked careful questions to help the manager perceive the full impact and scale of the problem. He then took a coaching approach to facilitating the solution. He wanted to the manager to arrive at a solution himself and was at pains to facilitate rather than provide answers."

Andy stated that the business outcome of these changes was acceleration in the delivery of critical projects but that it was the intangibles that were most impressive. The observable increase in confidence, communication and collaboration. The project management teams started listening and carefully working up solutions.

Robert did not try to enforce change from the top, rather he created an environment where the individual managers felt confident and empowered to drive the business. Robert's role was to remove the obstacles that stood in the way of success.

Robert also had a vision. In this vision he directed (not managed) a team of problem solvers and decision makers. His quiet questioning and facilitated problem solving helped the managers to develop, for themselves, the ability to assess a problem and formulate solutions.

www.ajpconsulting.org

There are many that believe state leaders are born and not made. I agree with the former but not the latter. I believe that by learning and applying some fundamental behaviours many (but not all) can become effective leaders.

Incidentally the natural leader is often identified as the one with a high degree of charisma and, while there are lots of examples of charisma as a core quality of great leaders, there are many examples of those without obvious charisma (Bill Gates, Michael Bloomberg, Gordon Brown).

I believe that the best evidence of a strong leader is an organisation where leadership is apparent and encouraged at every level; where there is a distinct lack of insecurity in leaders and where there are teams rather than groups.

I believe that the key to good leadership is to show the way and then get out of the way. Leaders that remove the obstacles that stand in the way of subordinates achieving success breed loyalty, independence of thought and innovative solutions.

In this example, Robert achieved business turnaround through inspiring and motivating the individual project managers.

The measure of the leader is the actions of their followers (the extent to which they gain an effective following), not the degree of charisma, charm, communication skills, etcetera.

I have heard inspirational leadership described as "leading by example" and "leading from the front". I have seen and heard about leaders who have gone out of their way to demonstrate the kind of behaviours that are required from the team.

1. Every year, at Christmas time, at a supermarket giant, managers work on the checkouts, stack the shelves and work side by side with the store staff.

2. At an investment bank, the senior managing directors leave no later than 2100 and make sure that they are the last person out of the office. They do this to demonstrate that a work-life balance is important to the firm.

3. The head of technology will support one technical bid every month to demonstrate commitment as well as keeping herself appraised of clients' needs.

4. At a famous military academy, officer cadets are drilled in the importance of leading from the front, literally leading the charge.

5. The general manager of a 150-bedroom hotel works the reception desk for an hour every week and demonstrates a passion for welcoming guests.

Case Study 24: Jamie

Jamie was one of my management team at a London hotel that I opened. He went on to lead hotels himself and he gave me the following story of inspirational leadership.

The few weeks leading up to the opening of a new hotel and then the first month after opening are pretty key moments in terms of getting the service offering right and embedding the right kind of behaviours and practices within the team.

On this occasion the hotel opening had gone really well. Staff morale was high, guest feedback was great (and by this we meant that we had received very few complaints and lots of compliments). As far as the owners were concerned, revenues were in line with expectations and there had been no exceptional costs.

He decided to conduct a team-building exercise to reflect on what a great job everyone had done. So he gave each department a sheet of paper and instructed them to write down three positive statements about each of their co-workers. This was to be done anonymously and as the General Manager he would compile the comments and give them out to the teams. It's a hugely motivational exercise. Each individual receives about thirty positive comments from their team. The exercise achieved its objectives and the team cemented relationships.

A side effect of this process was that several team members took the opportunity to write positive comments about the General Manager.

One individual's comments stood out from the rest on my desk.

"Jamie was everywhere. He had all of the answers and never seemed to lose composure. This gave us all confidence."

What a great example of inspirational leadership.

I am of the opinion that a large measure of professional will and a sense of personal humility are essential to demonstrating the humanity that followers seek in leaders. My interest in this sense of humility stems from an early brush with leadership literature with "Making it Happen, Reflections on Leadership" a short book by the chairman responsible for turning round ICI's fortunes in the 1980s. He listed among the traits of leaders, a profound sense of personal humility.

I realise that there are opinions that are contrary to this and that history has given us many examples of prominent leaders who do not immediately seem to have demonstrated humility (Margaret Thatcher, George W. Bush, Morgan Stanley's John Mack). However I am going to propose the importance of humility in demonstrating empathy and building integrity and trust.

The humble leader does not assume that they know everything but instead looks for people to explain things to them and learn from it. Much like the first example in this chapter, the leader enfranchises the team members into a shared sense of ownership and belonging.

Case Study 25: In the Stocks.

John told how he turned around a failing project by invigorating the team.

"We were developing what was essentially a fix to a legacy database that would enable the users to access client information that currently resided on a newer system. The fix was seen as hugely important for the business, speeding up the mean time to respond to client requests and reducing the number of data errors that came about as the result of incomplete or out of date data records. Unfortunately while I had been focusing on the senior stakeholders I had neglected the team. I knew that motivation was becoming an issue because there were increased occasions of late arrivals, individuals' attitudes to me as the project manager were changing and they became curt and a little evasive."

John went on to explain how he felt that this was an unfortunate side effect of not having sufficient resources to engage a stakeholder management or a team management specialist. A compromise that most of us will have experienced in projects to date.

"I decided it was time to get back in tune with the team, but it was going to be a tall order. Building morale in a new team is one thing but recovering it in an existing team is another. I decided to play on the fact that a shared enemy is a powerful motivational force and after some preparations I instructed the team to attend a mandatory team meeting on a Thursday afternoon at 1600 hours."

John had had himself photographed in stocks! He put the image into seven envelopes and had these sealed envelopes placed on the seats of the room that had been booked for the team meeting, written on the envelopes were the words, "Do not open until instructed to do so."

"I made sure that the team were in the room before I walked in myself. I walked straight up to the front and turned on the projector. Illuminated was a list of the deliverables and activities that I had requested of the team over the past four months. I started off by saying, 'I have asked a lot of you.' After a short pause I then said, 'I have also let you down by not giving you the support, the recognition and the time that you deserve. I would like to apologise, please open the envelopes on your seats and feel free to put these on your desks."

"There was some laughter so I followed up by saying, 'I've asked a lot of you I know that we need to work together to move forwards. I would like to invite you to ask of me what we need as a team to rediscover our vision, our mission and our sense of the team.' I provided a flip chart easel and pens and I asked them to workshop this for ten minutes while I left the room."

When John came back he found a list of requirements:

1. Approachable
2. Accessible
3. Supportive
4. Involved
5. Clear communication

John was able to use the rest of the time to create a team manifesto that incorporated what each member of the team needed to do to work in collaboration, to improve performance and to deliver the project. During the session John was careful to listen and to encourage the team members to make shared decisions.

"I was really concerned that the idea would fall flat, that no one would laugh and that I would lose all integrity. In actual fact it worked. What we have now is a sense of team. I have to be careful to make sure that I don't lose their trust and that I do what I say I will do. Regaining trust was hard, I'm not sure that the stocks would work if I lost it again."

Summary

Humility, defined by listening, not having the monopoly on good ideas, and sharing ownership breeds trust. Inspirational leadership is about transforming a vision into understandable media and then personally demonstrating through actual deeds and actions the behaviours and benefits desired in the future state.

Team building activities.

A team is defined by a shared objective and their efforts towards that end. A team differs from a group because they will work for each other. A team works collaboratively and in consideration of a purpose higher than individual achievement.

The change team can present the leader with a more dynamic set of challenges than a traditional operational team. The change team will be brought together for a specific purpose and once their objective has been attained the change team will disband. It may also be the case that the change team will grow and shrink at different times of the change initiative to accommodate specific contributors. The change team will include but will not be limited to the roles on the following page.

- o Sponsor
- o Change leader
- o Change support functions (PMO, task management, administration)
- o Direct contributors
- o Subject matter experts (SMEs) – functional and management, including risk, quality and cost management professionals
- o User representatives

The table below illustrates the changing nature of the team membership over the life-cycle of the change initiative.

	Initiate	Plan	Build	Test	Handover	Close
Sponsor	FULL	PART	PART	PART	FULL	PART
Change leader	FULL	FULL	FULL	FULL	FULL	FULL
Change support			FULL	FULL	FULL	FULL
SME	PART	FULL	PART	FULL	PART	
Contributors		PART	FULL	FULL		
Users			PART	FULL	FULL	PART

Table 11. The dynamic nature of the change team.

This table illustrates the changing nature of the change team as functions enter and exit the team. The challenge for the change leader is to anticipate the challenges that these changes will create and to plan activities to ensure that impacts are minimised and opportunities maximised.

Forming, Storming, Norming, Performing and Adjourning.

Originally developed in the mid-1960s, Bruce Tuckman added the adjourning stage to his model in 1970. Similarities can be drawn between this and other models of the time, specifically Hersey and Blanchard's situational leadership model.

Tuckman's model describes the stages that a team passes through as it matures. Students of this work understand the actions that a leader must take to safely navigate to the performing stage as quickly as possible.

- o Forming – There is little collaboration from the team members. Roles and responsibilities are unclear. The team relies on the leader for direction.

- o Storming – Team members vie for position relative to each other and the leader. Roles and responsibilities emerge but much uncertainty remains. The leader may be challenged. A focus on the team objective and purpose is essential to ensure that relationships do not distract.

- o Norming – There is a high degree of comfort around roles and responsibilities. The leader is able to delegate small tasks and facilitate team decisions. Commitment and unity is strong, the team may socialise and engage in fun activities together.

- o Performing – The team is self-sufficient. The team is aware of its objective and purpose. It actively agitates for delegated responsibility. Conflict and performance issues are identified and remedied within the team. The leader must be able to step back and remove the obstacles that stand in the way of the team performing.

- o Adjourning – The team is disbanding, hopefully with a sense of a job well done. However, strong feelings of loss may prevail as the individuals face an uncertain future after the change initiative. The change leader can plan for this and ensure that the team is able to celebrate success and are able to move on to anticipated next roles.

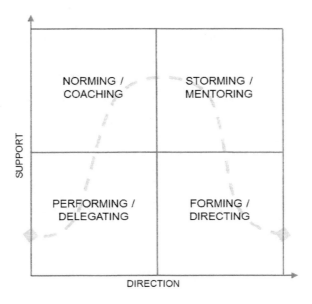

Fig. 12. Comparing and overlapping models

Figure 12 illustrates the relationship between the forming, storming, norming, and performing model and situational leadership.

Practically speaking

In the forming stage the leader is required to direct, in fact to do a lot of telling because the team or the team member is technically ignorant. Ignorant of the team charter, norms and behaviour but also ignorant of their role within that team.

As the team progresses into the storming stage the leader must continue to provide direction as the roles and responsibilities are learned but in addition to providing direction, the leader must start to support the team or team member. The leader aspires for their team to become self-directing, while achieving their objectives. There is an emphasis on mentoring in the storming stage, indeed it is worth noting that to proceed beyond storming requires the leader to give an increasing degree of autonomy to the team and for some leaders this may prove difficult.

At the norming stage, there is a reduction in the degree of direction required from the leader and this is in relationship to the competence of the team in achieving their role requirements and team objectives. As the team becomes more able, the leader is required to provide less direction. The degree of support remains the same or may in fact increase as the leader now provides coaching to the team and to the individuals. The objective of this stage is for the team to develop beyond competence and to be also confident.

Finally, at the performing stage, the leader has made themselves redundant in the role of directing and supporting the team. That is not to say that they have no further responsibilities, inputs or accountability but it is to say that now the team is confident and competent, it is advisable for the leader to step out of the way and let performance happen. Going forwards, this role of the leader as coach, mentor and director will be revisited as the team is required to adapt to changing objectives and changes in membership.

To elaborate on Tuckman's model there is a simple formula.

Operational team:

Confidence + competence + direction = performance.

However, the nature of a project team, referring back to Table 11, is that the team does not have the stability of static membership and therefore is prone to storming and norming. The formula for a project team needs to incorporate agility.

Project team:

Confidence + competence + direction + agility = performance.

In the beginning, at the start or kick off of a project the project team experiences excitement as they embark upon a new initiative. They will have some doubts that are manifesting about the uncertainty of the future, they will also feel a sense of togetherness as they embark upon a journey. In some respects we can liken the early stages of the project to a voyage of discovery where the crew of the vessel embark to explore unmapped territory.

If we followed this voyage analogy then we can see the group forming, excitedly discussing the challenges that lie ahead, revelling in each other's enthusiasm, masking strong personality differences and looking forwards, out to sea as the land diminishes aft. It will be shortly thereafter that reality dawns. Imagine periods of quiet and reflection as the individuals in the group start to contemplate their responsibilities, imagining now, not only excitement but also hardship and an uncertain future.

The captain of the vessel is now a key figure as he strives to keep the crew busy, because the captain knows that in activity the crew familiarises themselves with tasks as well as personalities. The captain knows that there will be conflict but he also knows that the crew needs to have an island of stability and he intends for that to be the mission, and the activities that make the mission a success. So the crew bend themselves to the tasks and activities of moving the vessel forwards and they familiarise themselves, becoming more adept at following instructions until the instructions become less and competence starts to take over.

The captain of the vessel recognises that this is the time for the crew to start taking more responsibility and so he starts to assign accountability for shifts on deck to individuals. He makes another individual responsible for cleaning the decks, another responsible for the changing of sails that can happen at regular intervals but requires precise teamwork. The group has started to grow as a team, a team reliant on the direction of the captain but proficient in carrying out their orders. They may not agree with the orders but there is familiarity with the tasks and there is a certain comfort even pride in doing a job well, to the satisfaction of the captain. Now that responsibilities are being clarified, roles and seniority established there is conflict, disagreement, resentment and outright denial.

The captain of the vessel has seen this before and knows that the best way to settle behaviour is to establish leadership through the supervisors and for there to be no further option. So the captain addresses the whole crew and formally acknowledges the new posts and responsibilities. He tells the crew that they can no longer address himself directly but through their supervisors. He congratulates them on their performance as a whole and encourages them to achieve harmony and performance as sub teams within the whole. At the end of his address the captain stands and for a moment surveys the crew, assembled on deck. He looks into the eye of every person present. He is careful to convey calm, confidence and authority because he knows that any question of frailty at this stage can sow the seed of a future mutiny.

The captain works closely with the supervisors, he sets them to task, he is utterly clear about their roles and responsibilities. He ensures that they have activities to perform with which they can become familiar, not the least of which is concern for the physical and mental health of their reports. He provides clear performance objectives but does not articulate the way in which they should be achieved.

The supervisors provide clarity of purpose and direction to their new reports, again giving an island of stability to their reports, the familiarity of tasks and contribution that will lead to satisfaction, normality and performance.

The crew must deal with obstacles, hardships and challenges. They will also have days of enjoying the sunshine gleaming off a calm blue ocean. When they are called upon to perform they will be absolutely clear about what is expected of them, the person that they are working next to or relying upon. They will listen to and respond to the instructions provided to them by those in authority.

This is a high performing team.

Imagine then what would happen if, at each port of call, several members of the team were replaced. In fact imagine if crew and supervisors experienced replacements and promotions.

The captain has seen this before and he knows from experience that this could mean a great deal of uncertainty, an impact on the overall cohesion of the team, a challenge to his leadership and a failure of the team performance. It could mean the captain spending large amounts of time directing, time that could be spent planning, strategising, navigating and achieving the voyage objective. So the captain instils a personal sense of ownership and contribution at every level of the crew.

The person responsible for cleaning the deck is not in fact cleaning the deck, they are contributing towards the overall goal of the voyage by ensuring a clean, safe and secure working environment. The person responsible for cooking breakfast for 70 crew members as the vessel corkscrews in uncomfortable seas is not cooking breakfast, they are contributing towards the overall goal of the voyage by ensuring that the crew is fed and has the energy to carry out their duties.

Not only are individuals responsible for their own contribution they are aware of the contribution of their fellow team mates and work together for each other. High performance by one member of a team reaps a reward for the whole team.

When the ship docks for the first time, the crew members left behind feel a natural sense of loss as their team mates leave to go on different vessels, to different locations. The crew also experience a sense of the unknown and of uncertainty as new crew members are introduced. Crew members that have not been through what the existing crew has. There are changes but the format remain the same, the tasks and activities remain the same, the requirement for individual and team accountability remains and so in a Pavlovian way, the new team members are enfranchised into the system. The existing team members incorporating them into the values, the tasks and activities, the teamwork and the shared ownership of the voyage goals and objectives.

In an environment where performance relies upon individuals in a team and in an environment where the team is likely to be subject to changing personnel then performance can be delicate. The wise, experienced leader will be aware of this and will mitigate this risk by embedding standards, direction and control while decentralising ownership for achieving the required performance levels.

Confidence + competence + direction + agility = performance.

Summary

It is not enough simply to understand that teams develop through life cycle stages. For the leader to promote and benefit from team performance they must understand the actions that are required to move the team effectively from storming and high direction to performing, low direction and low support.

In the sailing analogy and in other practical ways the leader anticipates the changes in the team dynamic and provides the catalyst for creating the change and the glue to embed it.

In conclusion, referring back to the opening notes. A team is defined by a shared objective and their efforts towards that end. A team differs from a group because they will work for each other. A team works collaboratively and in consideration of a purpose higher than individual achievement.

There are many activities that can be undertaken to achieve rapport and cohesion in the team however, it is the foundations of clear roles, objectives and contributions that will provide the stability to navigate and accommodate the unique challenges in the project team.

Empathy

In the previous section, we looked at team building. I illustrated the fragile nature of team performance as it navigates a path through the project life cycle, changes and a dynamic membership. Of course there are issues that can affect individual and team performance that have nothing to do with team dynamics. Tensions between team members, setbacks, personal issues and conflict. The pressure of deadlines once the euphoria of the launch has worn off. A project team member can be subject to conflict from the recipients of the change themselves as well as resource owners.

Sometimes these issues can be worked out within the team. In fact this would be the preferred and recommended route for leaders. If the team is able to remedy performance issues, to help an individual face and overcome problems then it only helps to strengthen their bond. Sometimes though, it requires an intervention from the leader and it is at these times that the ability to empathise with others comes to the fore. For the leader to be able to access emotional intelligence skills will mean that problems are identified earlier and their ability to deal with them will be enhanced.

142

If you have never experienced a specific feeling then it will be hard for you to imagine what another is feeling. The phrase "he/she can't relate to me" is very commonly applied in situations where empathy is lacking. If one person is feeling persecuted and the other has never experienced this feeling and the associated emotions then they absolutely cannot relate.

If I feel de-motivated and someone starts to describe to me how they would deal with my set of circumstances, to prescribe a solution or to offer a differing perspective from my own, I know that I will find that difficult. Unless that person happens to be in the same situation as me or, even better, has been in the same circumstances and has successfully navigated it.

We can all relate to the detachment that we feel when politicians from our national capital tells us how we should live our lives or make changes based upon some research or report that they have commissioned. A typical response would be, "what would they know?" or, "how could they possibly understand?"

Case Study 26: Greggs-gate

In March 2012, the UK government announced a new food tax in the budget. Previously hot food that had been sold under certain categories did not attract VAT. There was a debate as to whether food that was warmed for the customer such as pies and pasties, was "hot" and therefore subject to VAT.

A well-known and loved British bakery chain by the name of Greggs serves pies and other products that are cooked and maintained at a temperature that is neither too hot (to cause burning) nor too cold. An argument started about what "hot" was and in the end the official government line was that a product sold above room temperature or ambient temperature would attract VAT.

For Greggs this meant that the price of the products would have to be increased, in many cases above the symbolic £0.99 mark. For the ordinary person this meant paying an additional twenty pence for their product at no additional value.

The Prime Minister at the time was asked if he had ever had a pasty to which he replied that he thought that perhaps he had eaten a pasty from a railway station five years previously. By contrast the leader of the opposition was photographed in a Greggs shop purchasing a pasty. The politicians were attempting to demonstrate that they were not so different from the typical Greggs customer.

Empathy is about bridging a gap by demonstrating that not only do we understand the pain (sympathy) but that we have or are sharing that pain (empathy).

Empathy is variously described in the following terms:

o   The identification with and understanding of another's feelings.

o   Understanding and imaginatively entering into another's feelings.

As a leader we need to be able to do both. We need to be able to leverage our own experiences so that we can identify with what the other is going through and we need to be able to imagine what the other is going through if we have no direct comparison.

The objective of empathising with another is to gain a level acceptance of understanding and therefore trust. For the individual in crisis or suffering with de-motivation it might just be enough to know that someone else has been there and recovered successfully. This recognition that one is not alone is very important for self-esteem and is often the first step in returning to full emotional health and performance.

Practically speaking.

A director, working in the mergers and acquisitions area of a major investment bank joked to me recently, *"I operate an open door policy here, you can leave whenever the going gets too tough!"* This hard-nosed, performance-focused attitude is popular in high pressure environments but is also found in much wider leadership circles. The idea of using emotional intelligence skills, like empathy, is seen as "touchy feely" and frankly is "best left for those people in human resources."

Emotional intelligence, and empathy in particular, is a key skill in maintaining effective relationships and there is nothing touchy feely about it. In fact, many of the hard-nosed leaders that reject the idea of Emotional Quotient (EQ) are very empathetic. For example, they know when to throw in barbed comments about the performance of a sports team because they know how that will make the other person feel. They also know when to highlight the performance of an individual in a humorous way because they have experienced it themselves and they came out stronger. This is a basic use of empathy, understanding where others are, identifying with their position and likely feelings.

During the awful and frightening hours at the height of uncertainty on September the 11th 2001 the director responsible for the team that I worked in at the time told us that if anyone felt uncomfortable being in a tall building in central London they could and should leave immediately. We all did but there was no threat, in reality our building was only 11 stories tall and not in a particularly important part of the city but Chris recognised the sense of uncertainly and fear and acted. These were not the actions of a weak leader demonstrating touchy feely actions.

Remember Mike Golding, the skipper of the yacht Group 4 in the 1996 Global Challenge? Giving out Jelly Babies after every significant team action, specifically where the crew had pulled together to overcome an issue, wasn't a particularly big gesture but it was significant because Mike recognised the effort, the fear, the danger and the benefits of recognition. This was not a touchy feely action and this is not a touchy feely skipper.

To be able to empathise with others, there is one essential step that must be undertaken and that is to be open to one's own emotions. It is vital not to numb these feelings through denial, alcohol or ignorance. Our emotional intelligence learns from these emotions. In the same way as our practical competence improves with familiarity so does our emotional ability. From feeling, understanding these feelings and learning how to respond effectively to them we grow emotionally.

It is a normal part of life to suffer setbacks and disappointments. It is not the setbacks or disappointments that are significant, it is the way in which we respond to them that is significant.

The more feelings that we have experienced and acknowledged the more emotionally able we are to deal with their consequences. This is true but it is also true that I can then relate much more to the feelings and emotions of others.

It is a truism in sales that we don't buy products and services, we buy people. We buy people because we like them and, generally speaking, we like people because they are like us. The way we know that they are like us is because we can relate to them. I want to present two benefits of empathy:

1. The first benefit of empathy to a leader is that our team can relate to each other, creating a sense of belonging and trust, two steps on the road to empowerment and performance.

2. The second benefit of empathy is that team members and stakeholders will see in us characteristics and traits that they can relate to, believe in and trust. In short it can make us a leader that others want to follow.

Summary

Empathy is the oil of effective relationships. It is a lubricant that helps the project team get along well together. Empathy is a skill and tool that is worth developing. It is not touch feely but rather the ability to identify with, understand and relate to the feelings that another is experiencing.

The first time that I delivered a major keynote speech on camera (recording a video for International Project Management Day), I was so nervous that the day before I spent hours visualising my stance, articulating key points and maintaining a steady pace. On the morning itself I was still nervous and had to stop myself shaking. If you watch that video you would not see any of that nervousness. In part that is down to the video editing but also to the crew who calmed me down and assured me that everyone was nervous the first time but to enjoy the experience. I share that story with anyone that is preparing a significant presentation. Often the individual will retort, *"I can't believe that you get nervous."* I assure them that I do every time, even to this day, get nervous but that I have learned to harness that and I now enjoy myself. That's empathy and that's how it's used to build confidence, rapport and understanding.

Here are five practical actions to improve empathy.

1. Listen to others genuinely with ears, eyes and attention, oh, and don't interrupt them.

2. Tune into body language, yours and that of others. Is the verbal and non-verbal message consistent?

3. Remember names and facts. It shows that you paid attention and that the person was important to you.

4. Take an interest. Ask about interests, hobbies, home lives and encourage everyone to speak and share.

Get Intimate with the Team

This section builds on previous chapters, getting to know the wants and needs of stakeholders to manage their expectations. In this case it is the team members who are the stakeholders.

Case Study 27: Promotion

Hamish walked into the office impeccably dressed as always, in a dark blue suit, highly polished black shoes, a crisp white shirt with a starched collar and a tie that picked out the blue of the suit with a bold, diagonal, yellow stripe. His hair was neat and he wore fashionable, slim framed glasses that suited him well. I invited him to sit in a high back chair to my side so that we were sat facing each other not directly over the desk but less formally over a corner.

Despite Hamish's impeccable grooming that morning I could tell that he was nervous so I dispensed with the usual pleasantries and got straight to the point.

"Hamish, you asked to see me this morning. You said that you had something to clear up." As I said this I recalled his behaviour the previous evening when he had seemed agitated, frustrated, as if controlling a desire to express a strong emotion, to shout or stamp his foot. So I asked my question and then, with my hands placed visibly together on the desk I tried to remain still and calm so as to encourage Hamish to speak freely.

"I want to know why you promoted Trevor to team leader this week. I don't understand why I was overlooked. I want to know what my prospects

are here in this team." Hamish spoke clearly and without hesitation and I was relieved. In truth I had anticipated this and I welcomed the chance to resolve the issue with a man who worked tremendously hard and was very popular within the team for his work ethic, his positive demeanour and quick humour.

"I want to start out by saying that I completely understand where you are coming from." I started out speaking calmly and engaging Hamish with direct eye contact, being careful not to move my hands[12]. *"You have worked extremely hard on this project. You are a very valued member of the team. Your team mates rate you highly not only for your work ethic but for the way that you motivate and inspire others. If I were in your position then I would feel disappointed not to have been recognised with a promotion."* I paused to allow this to sink in for a moment and took the opportunity to offer coffee. Hamish declined but I got up and poured myself one anyway, before continuing.

"How are you feeling about this situation?" I had sat down again, with my coffee cup placed to one side and my errant hands now under control, once again.

Hamish had relaxed a little, though I could see something that looked like suspicion in his eyes. He responded quickly though and with an edge to his voice, *"I honestly feel let down, overlooked. I feel like all of my hard work is not recognised and that I should have been promoted. I feel de-motivated and disappointed."*

This was it, the key part. The crux, as climbers call it, the most difficult part of the discussion. If I were able to turn this around to overcome the issue, then the climb would be easier hereafter.

"I am glad that you have come to me this morning because I got this wrong and it's my fault that you are feeling let down, de-motivated and disappointed," I paused before continuing. *"I want to apologise for that because I too value your hard work, your contribution and the positive impact that you have on the team."* I paused again, waiting for what I had said to sink in. *"What I should have done was to explain to you why I had promoted Trevor but more importantly to explain to you that myself*

---

[12] My hands have a mind of their own and fidget without my noticing so I have to make an effort to keep them still!

and the project sponsor had discussed your contribution specifically and had agreed that you should be fast tracked."

Working hard to maintain my calm expression and body language I noticed with satisfaction that Hamish's expression had changed from cold and hard to interest and anticipation. I think that he even leaned forwards fractionally. In fact I was genuinely sorry and satisfied. What I said about the sponsor and I having spoken about Hamish was true, there was a plan of action. I was also sorry that in focusing on the promotion for Trevor I had overlooked the immediate impact on Hamish.

This time when I offered coffee, Hamish accepted.

"Hamish, you have demonstrated excellent attention to detail. You have led others and overcome issues and risks admirably. You have expressed for some time an interest in delivering change to a high standard. The sponsor and I therefore felt that we could benefit from you entering the Jump programme. Of course you would have to consider this and there would be no immediate pay rise but we felt that you had demonstrated the skills and qualities to become an excellent change manager and the Jump programme will give you that opportunity."

Hamish did not need a long time to think about this opportunity at all. We talked about the programme enthusiastically for ten minutes and enjoyed our coffee. We agreed the next steps and diarised an induction meeting for him. Before he went back to work I briefly explained why we had promoted Trevor, an individual who had been with the team a long time and had earned enormous respect from his peers but also had significant prior experience supervising others. Hamish accepted this completely, adding that Trevor would do a much better job that he would have been able to do himself.

Abraham Maslow in his 1943 paper summed up needs and wants pretty clearly with a hierarchy of needs. We might want a promotion, recognition or the admiration of others but if we haven't got a home, shelter, food or belonging then these higher aspirations are useless. Hamish wanted a promotion but he needed recognition.

Prime needs

I recall a survey conducted by the Institute of Directors in the early noughties that sought to understand what motivated individuals. The report cited three main motivators:

1. The organisational culture.

2. Recognition.

3. Pay and reward.

The organisational culture factor is the most important because the report went on to state and explain what was meant by organisational culture. "The actions and culture set by the leader" was the definition that was used for organisational culture. In the previous story about the manager in the stocks, John's formative actions were understood to be aloof and removed from the team as he focused on senior stakeholder management. This set the cultural actions and context for the team.

Going back to our list of three motivators. While I absolutely agree with culture being the prime motivator for a majority of people, having enough money is also essential, as I learned at an interview from a mentor and role model for me, Chris Garratt, the then Senior Director for Project Management EMEA at MCI WorldCom.

> *"What are your salary expectations, Adrian?"* Chris asked.

> *"Actually, Chris, it's all about the role for me. I'm more interested in the role than the money."* I responded.

With the benefit of hindsight, I cringe at the moment as Chris sat back and smiled.

> *"Adrian, money is always important. If I pay you one penny more than you need then you could be rich, but if I pay you one penny less than you need then you will not be able to focus on the job that I am asking you to do. So what do you need?"*

Maslow stated that motivation peaked when individuals achieved self-actualisation through problem solving, spontaneity, and achieving goals. However the pyramid that Maslow uses to illustrate his methodology also implies that each stage of motivation can only be applied once the underlying level has been achieved.

1. Level one is physiological – food, water, breathing, sleep.

2. Level two is safety – security of income, job, environment, the family and property.

3. Level three is belonging – friendship, family, love.

4. Level four is esteem – confidence, respect towards and from others.

5. Level five is self-actualisation - problem solving, spontaneity, and achieving goals.

Practically speaking

As leaders we need to ensure that our team members have sufficient of what they need to feel comfortable on the physiological and safety levels before we start giving them Jelly Babies, more responsibility or organising a team night out.

There are lots of motivational theories in mainstream leadership at present and all of them have traction.

o   Maslow's hierarchy of needs.

o   MacGregor's theory X and Y.

o   Herzberg's hygiene factors.

o   Adams' equity theory.

Each of these theories presents excellent ways to assess the motivational needs of individuals and I would recommend researching them all as they provide motivational levers. I want to expand simply on Adams' equity theory.

In a previous chapter I introduced the stakeholder chart. A model that builds upon our understanding of the wants, needs and contributions of our stakeholders and allows the leader to plan actions that create an equitable situation. The stakeholder will provide a contribution because there is something in it for them.

As a team leader we must assume that each individual is motivated differently and seek to establish what levers can be applied to create an equitable situation where team members will be prepared to contribute in a desirable way and then perhaps, what actions the leader and the team need to take to persuade the team member to perform beyond what is desirable, in short to go the extra mile.

For some individuals a Jelly Baby at the right moment will be the right thing, for another it will be regular and sincere recognition and feedback, another may be motivated by the sense of excitement and energy that comes from being part of something special, challenging or exceptional.

I encourage all of my workshop delegates to take time out at least once a week to review how well-motivated each team member is and to assess the effectiveness of the motivational techniques that have been applied. Of course I also think that while trial and error is important the best way to find out what motivates an individual is to ask them. In the earlier story John managed to turn around performance issues in the team by demonstrating humility and empowering the team. His question was simple, *"What do we need to do to turn this situation around?"*

Summary

I want to conclude by sharing a story of events at the end of a project that proved to be motivational and inspiring.

Case Study 28: Can you speak Swedish and Danish?

> The change initiative had been to consolidate six geographically diverse technical response call centres into one location in the City of London. The project had gone well but had done so against a backdrop that I would describe as negative towards structured project and change management. In short the organisation, while 20,000 employees large, still operated in an entrepreneurial way and many of the silo owners regarded the change process as a threat to their way of working. Project management was a title that had little meaning and projects generally were not well-publicised and when they were it was because they were failing or had failed.
>
> So the project had gone very well. The new teams had been brought together, property and infrastructure were in place and technically

sound, customers' expectations had been well-managed and the new call centre was ready to switch over on time and on budget.

Prior to go-live I had noticed that several of the key silo directors had been showing an enhanced level of interest in this project that looked as though it might be an unmitigated success. Positive comments started to come in and I recognised a subtle shift as senior individuals positioned themselves behind the project. Recognising this we quickly implemented a sooner than planned marketing and launch communication. In this we thanked senior stakeholders but we also made a point of thanking each member of the project team.

The go-live day was a busy one, as you could imagine, we were switching over from six different countries and were anxious that everything would work seamlessly. As the calls started to come through and faults were logged and acted upon the anxiety turned to celebration as the routing, systems and integration (not to mention the linguistic skills of our operatives) were proven.

That evening there was a celebration event. All of the project team and as many of the call centre staff that could come made an appearance, as did several of our newly enfranchised stakeholders. One or two of the senior directors spoke publically congratulating the team on the success.

As the evening wore on team members were smiling, laughing and congratulating each other. A wink here, a look there, a war story shared, a genuine sense of achievement. We started off this section with an outtake from the book, Global Challenge. Imagine being part of that adventure. As I reflect on that celebration party in London, back in 2001, I am mindful and ask, who would not want to be part of that party, having been part of that successful project?

As a footnote, the very next time that I was recruiting project team members I found that I had more volunteers than I could accommodate. Word had gotten out of this post-project celebration and created an enthusiasm for being part of the next project.

Motivating and inspiring the team isn't just about filling up a vessel with motivation it's about lighting a fire of shared objectives, togetherness and individual motivation then stoking it and keeping it burning throughout the change lifecycle.

One to One Reviews and Coaching.

It is typical of organisations to dedicate time to developing a spectrum of skills and competencies in an individual. Take a sales role, for example. You would expect to find negotiating, influencing, relationship building, communication, sales skills as key competences. We might also find 'core competences' in the role profile; integrity, passion, entrepreneurialism and so on. Typically an organisation would dedicate time and resources to ensure that an individual was able to demonstrate a basic level of competence against all of these requirements, thereby making a rounded individual.

For reasons that I will explain next, I believe that in a project environment this is undesirable and wasteful. I will argue that the project leadership team should provide developmental resources for those competences that an individual uses to contribute towards the project's success[13].

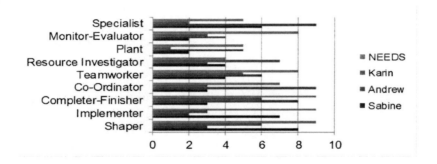

Fig. 13. Belbin team types and profiles.

The work done by Meredith Belbin and published in 1981 in the formative book Management Teams, Why They Succeed or Fail is widely read and understood as a guide to employing and developing those skills necessary to meet the requirements of a team environment. I

---

[13] The individuals should have been recruited with a specific role and qualities in mind.

would like to apply it to the skills and qualities that my research has identified as key to a successful project.

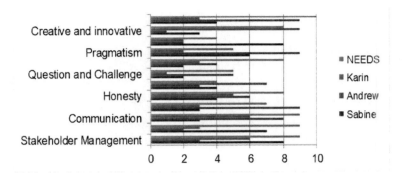

Fig. 14. Project team types and profiles.

What both of these tables illustrate is the fact that:

1. No one person possesses all of the skills and qualities required to successfully deliver projects.

2. The combination of skills and qualities represented by the team must meet the project requirements.

3. It would be logical to assign responsibilities according to skills and preferences[14].

Previously I said that I would propose not developing rounded individuals, rather focusing on developing specific skills and qualities. I will expand on that now in the next case study.

---

[14] I use the term preferences as an assumption. I assume that if individuals have a skill or a talent and manifest a high degree of competence in that area then this represents a preference.

Case Study 29: The Heartbeat of a Team.

In October 2009 Jenson Button became the Formula 1 World Champion for a brand new team, Brawn GP. The next year Button joined Lewis Hamilton on the McLaren F1 team, a move that attracted a great deal of interest.

How would Button compete with Lewis Hamilton, the 2008 Formula 1 World Champion, in a team that had been "built around" his team mate Lewis Hamilton, who is widely accepted to be the fastest out and out racer in Formula 1 at that time?

In the first season, Jenson Button finished in 5th place, 26 points and one place behind Lewis Hamilton.

In his second season for McLaren, Jenson Button finished second in the World Championship, 43 points and three places higher than his team mate, Lewis Hamilton.

To understand how this happened requires a deeper understanding of what else Jenson Button brings to the team. Button is a communicator, he is also a networker and works hard to build up sophisticated relationships with his engineers and the team technologists. He is known for providing detailed feedback on the performance of the car and working closely with his engineers to get the best out of his car.

The team principal, Martin Whitmarsh has, I imagine, two very different challenges in getting the best out of his drivers. For Jenson Button it is to provide him with the team that he can work with that will enable Button to use his communication skills to get the best performance on track. For Lewis Hamilton it is to provide him with a car that enables him to express his undoubted talents on the race course and win races.

In an organisational context there might be a temptation to develop the communication, feedback and relationship building skills in Lewis Hamilton, thereby enabling him to benefit to the same degree as Jenson Button does. To do so however misses the point entirely. Hamilton can no more be a superb communicator than Jenson Button can become the world's fastest out and out racer. I suggest that it is better to develop further the existing abilities of these drivers that reflect their preferences. In short, I propose playing and coaching to their strengths.

Defining Coaching.

At its heart, coaching is about releasing inner potential and not showing the way, the latter is more like mentoring. A coach will help the coachee to find their own path by asking insightful questions and helping the individual to order their thoughts. I often hear a coachee say, "I know what you are doing, you are trying to get me to answer my own question!" Absolutely right, I say.

o A coach is someone who should hold a coachee accountable for their values.

o A coach is someone who should challenge an individual to live out their potential.

o A coach is someone who should push, stretch and make the coachee think.

Case Study 30: Becoming a Carpenter.

There is a difference between learning to build a chair and learning to become a carpenter.

Steven is doing an apprenticeship with a master craftsman, a carpenter with over thirty years' experience. At the beginning of his apprenticeship, Steven spends a lot of time sweeping the floor of the workshop and cleaning the various saws, chisels, lathes and other tools of the carpentry trade. Steven learns the importance of each piece of equipment, how to assemble it, its uses and its dangers.

Next Steven is given tasks to perform that contribute to the finished piece. He learns to cut, to mitre and to sand to a fine finish. Steven learns the importance of precision, patience and attention to detail.

Over the coming years Steven learns about different joints, brackets, hinges, cuts and cornering. Eventually Steven is given whole pieces of furniture to complete. In the beginning he will seek guidance on specific pieces that are new to him but on the whole he has the confidence to start and complete every job.

By comparison, Marcus learns to make chairs. In his first few weeks he is shown how to build a chair. He is instructed in the use of the tools specific to making chairs. He watches, learns and is guided in the process of making beautiful dining room chairs from a variety of hard woods. Over the coming years, Marcus becomes an expert chair maker and is as quick, efficient and delivers high a quality product as anyone else in the workshop.

What is the difference between these two individuals now? Whereas Marcus has learned how to make chairs, Steven has become a carpenter.

If we teach people how to make chairs then if the time comes to make a table then they will have to come to us and ask us to show them how to build a table. If, however, we teach people to evaluate methods, understand tools and have confidence in themselves then we set them free to develop their repertoire.

Strength-Based Coaching (SBC)

I came across the concept of SBC when I was researching a coaching workshop for a UK insurance firm. They had expressed a desire to learn more about SBC and conduct two workshops with their line managers.

At the time there was very little in the way of research into SBC. There was some published American research into how effective it was to focus on the strengths of athletes and to develop their strengths. There was also Strengths Finder (2007), the book by Marcus Buckingham that helps individuals to identify their strengths but very little else.

SBC focuses on helping an individual to achieve their potential by developing their strengths but at the same time minimising the impact caused by their weaknesses.

Performance = Potential – Interference.

A simple example is where an ace sales person is held back by their poor ability to comply with the administrative burden of their job. In short, this person is superb in front of the prospect but fails to complete the order forms correctly, resulting in late delivery, cancellations and other evidence of poor customer satisfaction. This situation gets the sales person down who tries harder, spends more time on the administration part of their role at the expense of selling. The result is that instead of improving customer satisfaction the sales person generates less sales but makes little difference to overall customer satisfaction. If we were able to remove the need for this sales person to complete the sales documentation and release them to focus entirely on sales then they would be a high performer, playing to their strengths.

The fundamental question to ask then is this:

"If you are to become a top performer in your area of expertise, which skills do you need to develop to world class and which skills, qualities or tasks need to done by someone else?"

Tips For Effective Coaching:

1. Contract the coaching intervention. Coaching only works well when the individual wants to be coached and sees a benefit. So what's in it for them?

2. Find an appropriate time and place. There is nothing worse than feeling rushed when coaching is about listening in a calm and comfortable environment.

3. No surprises. Manage expectations and discuss what will happen during the intervention with the individual.

4. Prior preparation. Consider a tool like GROW (Goal, Reality, Options, Will) and use a template to ensure that you can stay on track as the coach. Prepare some opening, high-gain questions like, "Describe your ideal next 12 months."

5. Set the scene. State the duration of the intervention and remind the coachee that it is all about them achieving their goals. You are there to help them not to direct them.

6. Stay on track. Listening is hard and the temptation to interrupt can be terrible but follow the (GROW) plan and provide the coachee with the opportunity to find their own path.

7. Agree actions. A coaching intervention without stated, measurable actions is just a chat.

8. Follow up.

GROW

GROW[15] is one of the most common coaching tools and provides a framework to deliver a meaningful result.

Goal – Where does the coachee want to be? Objective, outcome, ambition, etcetera. The purpose is to get the coachee to describe this future state in a clear and measurable way.

- o   Q. How will you know when you have reached your goal?

- o   Q. How would you describe success?

Reality – Often the biggest challenge is overcoming the perceived problems that are faced in reality. The purpose is to help the coachee to challenge and describe the reality not as they see it, but as it really is.

- o   Q. Explain what is stopping you from achieving your goal?

- o   Q. Would a peer see this reality the same as you?

Options – There are always a range of options available to overcome every issue and so the objective of the coachee is to explore them. This can be challenging for the coachee who may have struggled with a difficult reality for some time. Once the options have been explored the coach may then help the coachee to prioritise and select an appropriate course of action.

- o   Q. Tell me, how can this problem be overcome?

- o   Q. How would you go about evaluating and prioritising amongst these options?

Will - The will to commit to a course of action. The entire coaching intervention comes down to what happens at this stage. The coach must gain a commitment to action from the coachee. A commitment to carry out the actions identified in the previous stage.

- o   Q. What will you do now?

---

[15] There is no definitive conclusion on the authorship of the GROW model though it is referenced widely in coaching literature.

o   Q. How will you measure the success of your actions?

Summary

In combination with active listening, coaching can be the most rewarding intervention for a leader. The joy of listening to someone overcoming a problem himself or herself. The moment when the coachee realises that they have identified the course of action to move forwards to their goal is truly inspiring.

Strength-based coaching focuses this coaching effort on enabling an individual to develop strengths and minimise weaknesses as part of a multi-functional team.

As a project leader, coaching is personally and professionally rewarding as it will result in empowered individuals contributing positively towards the project objectives by playing to their strengths.

Employing active listening.

Referring back to the example of the case study at the beginning of this chapter, one of the things that Robert did to make a cultural shift from "I" to "We" was to consistently listen. It is popularly said that in making crucial decisions, great leaders will always allow the contributors to speak first, thereby giving themselves all of the input but also engendering a sense of collaboration.

When we employ active listening it makes the speaker feel valued, it encourages collaboration and sometimes it facilitates a fascinating learning journey.

Case Study 31: Just Say No!

I met Fraser on a preparation workshop that I was running for the Project Management Professional Examination. Fraser delivered high value, complex and challenging infrastructure projects for a national rail company. Fraser told me that the projects were challenging because of the demanding nature of his client. He asked me how I would deal with a situation where the client would change their mind and demand compliance without formal change control or scope change notification. I asked Fraser to describe the situation to me.

"What we have is a client that is used to getting their own way." Fraser explained. *"They will arrive at a meeting and interrupt my progress report to say that instead of signalling being placed at the original height that they were changing the specification based upon an internal report."* Fraser described how the client felt able to demand changes with impunity.

At this point Fraser stopped talking and looked at me. I sense that he wanted me to say something but I also sensed that he was able to resolve this one himself so I said nothing. In fact I tried to remain as still as possible, with my hands folded in my lap and maintain eye contact. After probably 30 seconds Fraser started talking again.

"I tried saying no but they go over my head to the programme manager. I talked to the programme manager and they said that if they say no the client goes over their head to the operations director and at that point the operations director says something like, 'why am I being bothered by a £25,000 change, just do it.'"

Again I tried to remain still and maintain eye contact. This time Fraser started talking again, only after a short pause.

"Of course the answer is to have a consistent message up and down the organisation." Fraser smiled and paused for a moment before continuing, *"the problem is not with the client is it? The problem is that the operations director says yes."*

I smiled and this time opened my mouth to congratulate him on identifying the root cause of the problem. *"What are you going to do about it?"* I asked.

"We need to get the Ops Director in a room and get him on board. He needs to say no!"

I have had the privilege of observing this process many times and each time it pleases me enormously because the individual, the coachee, has learned the most valuable lesson, how to approach and resolve problems.

Practically speaking

From a practical point of view, active listening is about encouraging the speaker to continue speaking and for them to feel valued, listened to and then to start using these opportunities to vocalise and resolve problems.

In short the active listener becomes a sounding board and boards can't talk!

Posture, eye contact, stillness, a slight inclination of the head all of these things help the speaker to feel encouraged.

Active listening is hard because the brain can work so much faster than speech and so it becomes distracted. The brain starts to process other activities, sometimes thinking about the next meeting, an overdue item on the to-do list and at other times the temptation to stop the individual and tell them the answer becomes almost overpowering. If that is the case, stop. Don't do it!

If I ask you to talk but then I keep interrupting you and giving you the answers what am I actually saying to you?

I'm saying, *"I don't really want to listen to you and I know better."*

It doesn't seem like that and I may be really well-intentioned but interrupting and mentoring are not great examples of active listening.

One final piece of practical advice and this is directed towards those individuals who really like to talk and would potentially take up your entire day talking if they could. Don't avoid them, seek them out regularly and ask them to explain something to you. Listen for a few minutes and then gently raise your hand in a stop signal. If that doesn't work then say their name. This should stop them. Thank them for their input, tell them that it was really valuable and then tell them that you must immediately go and write it down, consider fully what they have said or implement the outputs. It has got to be sincere but it works.

Conclusion

1. Identify when an individual wants to talk and give them the attention that they need.

2. Listen without prejudice and be encouraging.

3. Amazing things can happen when individuals are encouraged to speak.

Prepare to adapt and update your leadership approach to meet individual preferences.

Lesson Eleven:

See Good, Hear Good, Speak Good

Chapter Thirteen: The Power of Personal Presence

I can tell what you are thinking! Well, mostly. Generally, when I'm addressing a group of people I can do a simple trick of mind reading, as follows:

o   10% of the audience are thinking about food; not enough breakfast, too much breakfast, lunch, dinner, mid-morning snack, etcetera.

o   5% are thinking about a leisure break of some sort, be it a holiday, the weekend activities or an exciting evening.

o   20% are thinking about something that another speaker or person said that day: the boss, the previous presenter, a partner, the parking attendant.

o   30% are thinking that their seating position is not ideal but they are not about to move just yet so as not to draw attention to their plight.

o   50% are thinking about work; projects or emails.

o   At least one of us is hoping that the others are with him ... of course that person is me!

I have this dream. I have this dream where project managers take a seat alongside legal and finance at the high table of organisational decision-making. I have this dream that project managers are respected drivers of organisational profit through the effective management of organisational development and change.

Unfortunately where we are is on the other side of a wide and deep chasm from where we want to be but the good news is that we are project managers and so we know how to construct a plan and build a bridge. The building blocks of this bridge are based upon our ability to empathise with our stakeholders, build rapport with influencers and decision makers, become part of the business development programme not the business prevention department. Project managers must recognise that methodology, control and systems are not the only way to deliver change but through a blend of leadership, communication, influencing and control. If we are to build this bridge then we must be listened to seriously and to for that to happen we have to understand the what, the why and the how of presence in our actions and activities. In short what we are looking at is a revolution and revolutions always start with an inspirational ideal and an inspirational leader.

At the conclusion of this chapter I want you the reader to think about the way in which we deal with personal situations more clearly and to go away and create a way of getting into the room, being present, in the here and now.

I am going to start off with some background to describe presence, what it is, why it matters and then move on to describe four key ingredients to effective presence:

1. Being congruent.

2. Communicating consistently through the message, body language, tone and vocabulary.

3. Empathising and building rapport.

4. Being present in the present.

Mr President

Pick a president, any president. You can probably switch this for any prime minister, country leader and definitely for business leaders. Why are they in this position of power, I ask you? Is it because they are the most qualified, most experienced, most embedded in the politics, community, business understanding? Largely actually no, they are not.

I used the example of a president because in my perception, presidents generally seem elected on their ability to inspire a following through the various primaries and speaking appointments. Here in the United Kingdom there's less of that and we as voters are encouraged to vote for policies that are supported through a network of local members of parliament.

Have you heard Barack Obama speak? There is a lot of material of his speeches, the one that I use for illustration purposes is the one back in January 2008 at the New Hampshire Primary. It's brilliant speech writing because it's inclusive. Find a transcript and look at how many groups, ethnicities and peoples he references in the first few paragraphs. Brilliantly inclusive, he brings it all together and talks about "us" and "we" and "our change" and "our dreams". It's not the words that I want to draw attention to it's the way in which he delivers the words, the pauses, the articulation; it's his use of body language, the way in which he reinforces what he is saying with his posture, his facial expressions, his tone and pace and his eyes. I am transfixed and I absolutely believe that he is going to do what he says he is going to do.

The same can be said of all great public speakers; it's just that North American politicians do it so well.

The interviewee

Picture yourself prepared to interview someone for a senior position. Clearly you have done your homework and you have scripts, questions, behavioural response measures; you've read this person's curriculum vitae and you have penned some searching questions.

You take a deep breath and then go out to meet your candidate.

Opinions vary but it is generally agreed that the impressions made within the first three seconds to the first five minutes of meeting a new person are unlikely to be heavily changed by subsequent interactions. So you walk out to meet your candidate and your first impressions are of someone who wears sharp but not overstated business dress, sports sensible and well-coiffed hair, has an upright posture, carries a business briefcase and polishes their shoes to a high shine. You are impressed and already your demeanour is changing because you want this person to be the manifestation of what your bias is telling you they should be based upon these first impressions.

Albert Mehrabian, in 1976 suggested that 93% of communication was non-verbal with 53% of it being based on body language and facial expression. When you say hello and introduce yourself the candidate smartly stands, extends a hand, flashes a modest but winning smile, calmly introduces themselves with flawless diction and exchanges a firm handshake. You are impressed by a firm handshake and the delicate and intoxicating blend of confidence and servility impresses you further. You are thinking to yourself, 'It's early, but this is a promising start.'

Of course being a professional you pull yourself together and take control of the situation and, after setting the scene you ask the first of your probing questions. The problem is that when the person speaks you listen; not just to what they are saying but how they are saying; you are convinced and agree entirely with what this person is saying. It's hard to describe but they have this certain something; it's in their eyes, their calm but expressive demeanour; in the way that they express their logic that seems to fit exactly with your worldview. They seem utterly believable, a person with integrity that will surely do what they say they will do.

It's possible that you haven't experienced this phenomenon, but if you are alert to it you will start to notice people with presence.

What is presence?

In the 4th century BC Aristotle described communication and presence as the ability to:

1. Present logical arguments.

2. Demonstrate a commensurate degree of appropriate emotion.

3. Project integrity through their character.

Presence is hard to describe but you know if you've got it or if someone else has got it because from the moment that you are in the room with them, you listen to what they are saying, laugh when they laugh, answer questions when they ask them, smile when they smile and miss them when they are gone.

For the purposes of a definition, presence is the state of fact of being present, in immediate proximity in time or space.

Why presence matters.

You may recall that I started this chapter with a challenge, a valley to cross and a bridge to build. I also stated earlier on that revolutions do not often start without an inspirational vision and an inspirational leader.

- o Che Guevara
- o Martin Luther King
- o Napoleon Bonaparte
- o John Adams
- o Karl Marx
- o Emmeline Pankhurst

All of these individuals had the personal presence to inspire a following and make change happen.

Presence matters because it is the ability to be in the room, in the moment and to gain the opportunity to inspire and influence others, be it in a change situation, a job interview a supplier negotiation or a stakeholder conversation.

So far, I've described presence as the state of being present and the ability to inspire and influence others. I've illustrated this with some examples of situations where presence can make a huge difference, in politics and in an interview scenario. Let's now look at the first of those four ingredients, congruence.

Being congruent.

Congruence is easier to spot when people and organisations are not doing it well; such as an organisation that has as its marketing slogan, "Looking after the little people" but is then exposed for using sweat shops in the developing world. We are all familiar with the huge breach of fiduciary trust carried out by banks in the early 2000s as organisations whom we trust for fiscal prudence bankrupted themselves with an unwise, unsafe and greedy financial apparatus.

I'm sure that many of us have had a poor experience trying to speak to someone in customer service about a faulty product or service after having been promised gold-standard support following a purchase.

Simply put, congruence is doing what you say you will do and reinforcing the message with every action and manner.

The open door policy.

We have all heard of or experienced, with varying degrees of positivity, the open door policy. It's usually couched along the lines of, "My door is always open, come in whenever it suits you or when you need me."

The problem is that, despite good intentions, for many managers that's just not practical because of the demands of their jobs. So when the individual does come to the boss's office they can often find that the door is not in fact open or, if it is, that now is not a good time.

How refreshing and inspiring is it then when the boss says, "Actually now is not a good time, but I will come and find you in 15 minutes," and then actually does do that, apologises for not being available and then gives that person their undivided attention to the matter in hand?

There are couple of considerations here:

1. By keeping the communication channel open, the boss is kept in the loop.

2. The employee will feel confident and empowered to approach the boss next time, for better or for worse.

3. By demonstrating a commitment to the individual the boss imparts value and worth.

Richard Branson stated that there are three sets of stakeholders that he needs to satisfy to make a business successful:

1. Shareholders

2. Staff

3. Customers

He maintained that his focus was staff because if the staff were motivated that they would satisfy the needs of customers (at a profit) who in turn would satisfy the needs of the shareholders. In terms of presence this is a great lesson in empathy, being present and congruent.

Incidentally, I'm not a champion of the open door policy. It might be my personal preference but it doesn't work in all environments. The point is to be consistent, not to be accessible; if the boss's position is that they are not available from 0800 until 1300 daily and they maintain that behaviour then it is consistent and it is congruent with their brand.

When congruence fails, when observers identify conflicts and inconsistencies between what an individual or organisation is saying and what it is doing the observers start to lose faith. It's beyond this point that no amount of inspirational communication or declarations of reinvigorated commitment will work. It falls on deaf ears.

I'm an organised guy, really!

How's your desk looking? Mine is populated by staking systems and sports many drawers and folders. I'm the kind of guy that does lots of things, not necessarily at the same time but I keep a lot of plates spinning. My desk probably reflects this. It would be incongruent of me to state that I was a highly disciplined person or worse a completer-finisher. I'm not and very little about my personality suggests that. Ironically I sometimes like to think that I am, so imagine the mixed messages that the observer would get if chatting with me by my desk and I was advocating the clear desk policy.

Summary

"All the world's a stage and all the men and women merely players. They have their exits and their entrances and one man in his time plays many parts."

Thus spake Shakespeare. I believe that from the moment we enter the fray at work or play that we must consider the image, the brand and the values that our actions, personality, dress and behaviour project. Are they congruent with the messages that I am articulating? Am I doing what I say I am doing because if I am people will trust me and listen to what I am saying.

Body language

Earlier I quoted Mehrabian whose research argues that 93% of communication is non-verbal, that is to say it is based not on what we say but how we say it and how those messages are communicated through our physical actions and facial expressions.

"I have done nothing wrong…"

A prominent business leader takes his company down an acquisition route, merging with a competitor in the biggest deal of its kind in the history of the sector. The share prices goes north and our leader is feted in the media as a visionary. Later that same year the share price has gone south and it would seem that a lack of due diligence is to blame for a massive miscalculation and gross overvaluation of the merger partner's stock.

The business leader is bullish and is interviewed in a live debate. The discussion starts comfortably with gentle questions about the background to the deal which the business leader is happy to take and argues positively; one would remark that his body language was open and honest with wide expressive and inclusive gestures. However, when the discussion turns to probing about due diligence and the interviewer targets specific questions the business leader's body language changes and there is a conflict between what he is saying and the message that we can read from his body language. He is saying, *"We did everything according to our processes and in line with industry standards. We still believe that the value is there and that in the coming weeks we will expose the synergies and advantages brought about by this merger.*" Throughout this exchange the business leader looks uncomfortable with closed gestures, wringing of hands and general small movements or fidgets. What his body language is saying is, *"I really don't like answering these questions and I don't wholeheartedly believe in the answers that I am giving."*

One week later the business leader, the founder of the organisation is forced to step down and is replaced.

This links back to the previous point about congruence. There is a disconnect between what the speaker is saying in words and what their body is saying. At best this creates unease, at worst the observer will lose faith and confidence in the speaker.

"I am going to support you 100%," says the voice but the speaker is not maintaining eye contact and they have got their hands in their pockets. Contrast this with a story I read about a famous Italian general working in Sicily in the early 80s at the height of Mafia intimidation. His police chief in Palermo was fearing for his life and so the general came to Palermo and he walked, arm in arm with the police chief past the homes of suspected Mafia enforcers. *"I am going to support you and walk beside you 100% of the way."*

I observe lots of people listening and talking. By far the most impressive people are the ones who are able to listen intently, without movement, eyes alert and focused, head tilted slightly to one side. Most people can learn to be expressive when talking and articulating a vision. It's the calm presence that is much more difficult to achieve; being there, actively listening and encouraging the other person to engage is very powerful and the greatest illustration of presence in terms of body language.

Summary

The topic of body language is closely linked to that of the previous section, congruence. Consider how to support what you are saying in words with deeds and with actions and with body language.

Empathise

So far in this section I have described ingredients that should result in the sense of character or integrity that Aristotle was proposing in the 4th century BC. Congruence in actions, body language and in behaviours creates trust and belief in others. In this section I would like to look back at an ingredient that I explored earlier, one that will make others want to listen, to follow and to support: empathy.

Put yourself in someone else's shoes…

Imagine that you have done well at school and university and that you are feted by global organisations promising you phenomenal rewards in return for your services and talents. They throw tinsel at you and buy you champagne and entice you into entering into a graduate contract.

For the first six months you are treated like the future leader of tomorrow. You are put up in a five-star hotel along with other similarly bright young minds and you are given the best training that money can buy, every evening you are entertained and treated like the success that you are.

The next two years you work long hours, very long hours indeed, you sleep little but you are part of something, something special. In fact you are changing that way in which the world economy works and in doing so you are making a lot of people very wealthy. You are part of wealth creation and you are being well paid, not that you get much time to spend it. Everyone that you work with is busy, they are well-dressed, they are ambitious and they are successful. Soon you are taking taxis to and from work, bypassing public transport because work is paying.

You reach your fourth year, you are a senior analyst, you see only success surrounding you and you can see only up. In fact for ten years the only market that this sector has seen is up. Then a terrible thing happens, the foundations of your world are rocked because assumptions are proving unfounded and the unthinkable is happening and the very future of your world is in doubt. Credit derivatives are toxic, homeowners in America are defaulting and subprime securities are spiralling out of control and you are staring at a downward spiral for this first time in ten years.

Suddenly everyone is talking about you for the wrong reasons. They are saying that you are a crook and that you have created a recession and that you are bad to the core, even though you don't actually work in credit derivatives, in synthetic trades or even in an investment bank, you work in the corporate part of a global bank.

For reasons beyond your control your bonus is cut, hundreds of your colleagues are fired and the future of your career is in doubt; even within your bank the very behaviours that were encouraged six months earlier are vilified.

Can you empathise with this banker? Can you walk even one step in their shoes, for even a moment can you feel their anxieties and fears? If you can do this, take that tiny step, then how much easier it must be to step into the shoes of a supplier, a team member, a stakeholder or business representative and understand their anxieties, fears and goals.

Empathy is demonstrating to the other person or persons that you understand them, that you are in their corner and that the two of you are in it together. If you recall the speech that I quoted earlier by Barack Obama at the New Hampshire Primary, you may have read it and noticed how many groups, minorities and interests were incorporated in to the opening section of the speech. Obama demonstrates empathy, he knows what it is to be a steelworker, a housewife or a street cleaner and he collects all of these groups together and shares their vision for change with his own – we all want change and it is coming to America!

Summary

There is a commonly-held misconception that to be liked and interesting is to do nice things and to talk about interesting things when in fact, to be liked and interesting generally means to be interested in the other person, what they like. The most interesting person is the most interested person.

Be in the present

This final ingredient is the most difficult one. I touched on it earlier on when I said that those practitioners of active listening have my most humble and profound respect. I also referred to that empathy skill of being genuinely interested in someone else's likes and interests.

Have you seen the Dalai Lama speak? I haven't either but I am curious. It's not out of a profound desire to understand more of his teaching, though I find a lot to like in the buddhavacana, it's more to experience the presence of a man, a small man, who can captivate an audience of tens of thousands. On the 15th August 1999 forty thousand people crowded in to Central Park to hear the 14th Dalai Lama speak about compassion. I met a woman who was there, she was a delegate on a PMP course that I was running for an investment bank in London. She maintained that at even at a distance of several hundred metres, his presence was captivating. Do you get that? Can you understand that?

If you are worried that I might start quoting verse or chanting right now it's okay, I won't, but clearly he does. In fact most public speakers and presenters will have a ritual that they follow before they start, before they come on to stage. I'm right aren't I? Some of you will relate to that if you've not done much public speaking.

Case Study 32: Monkey Boy

Steve Balmer, ex-Microsoft chief executive became as famous for his over-zealous presentations as for his business leadership and decisions. There are many YouTube clips of Mr Balmer delivering presentations, one of them is entitled Monkey Boy, do you know that one? Have you seen it? It's quite amazing and it polarises audiences because many people like it and many are repelled by it. He is jumping around the stage, literally jumping and bouncing and shrieking, waving his arms around and hollering to a track by Gloria Estefan. It's worth a peek and after maybe forty seconds of this cavorting he leans on the lectern and pants, out of breath, *"I have four words for you - I love this company."* The crowd love it, they go wild.

Now I've seen this in the flesh; not Steve Balmer sadly, because I would love to see the man, he's got such energy and definitely has presence, no rather I have seen this kind of thing. In 2003 I was responsible for opening the Express by Holiday Inn in Stratford, East London and I went on a leadership development programme all about inspiring and motivating. I entered the room which was set out sort of like a classroom. There was a stage at the front flanked by two large pop-up banners with a lectern stand and a very large projector screen at the back. I sat down in the middle of the auditorium. Well you would, wouldn't you? The middle is a safe place to be, not too close to the front but close enough to be involved while being not too far from the exit. The room was set up for probably around 100 people and within a few minutes all of the audience were at their desks.

What happened next was quite mesmerising; I recall that there was some music and there was an announcement introducing the host but all of this is a bit sketchy because what happened next burns so brightly in my consciousness that everything else seems grey by comparison. From the wings jumped, yes not walked or entered, jumped a man onto the stage in what I could best describe as a star jump. He landed in front of the lectern with wide eyes, a sharp suit, arms raised like an evangelist and he shouted, *"I am here, how are you all doing!"* He might not have actually shouted but in my reeling mind it was loud and brash and in my face and I was mesmerised. My body reacted instantly and I pushed back in my seat. I think in hindsight that this was the flight reflex at being presented with this threatening behaviour. I recall two other things about that interlude, one was the behaviour of the other delegates: half of them had experienced an almost identical reaction to mine and were physically pushing backwards away from the speaker but the other half were leaning in. Classic emotional response behaviour and fascinating in its own right. The other thing was that the speaker held his pose for a full five seconds or so before relaxing his whole demeanour.

"Seriously though," he spoke quietly and carefully, *"how are you all doing? I imagine that I shocked quite a few of you there? I want to talk to you about how to gain and maintain the attention of your audience."*

Outstanding theatre and an afternoon that I enjoyed and learned a great deal from.

He went on to explain that before he goes on stage he looks in a mirror and makes himself laugh. It relaxes him and puts him in the right frame of mind.

Have you seen live comedy? Have you listened to a comedian that has had you in stitches, laughing out loud? If you have then try and think

www.ajpconsulting.org

back and answer me this question: are you in any way thinking about your BlackBerry, emails, agenda, tomorrow's early start? No, of course not and that's because laughter happens at the emotional level and is more powerful than the feelings that drive more fleeting thoughts like the fifty things on our to-do lists.

Laughter allows the speaker, me and many other contemporaries to get into the now, to be present in the present, in the room.

Of course humour is far from the sole emotion required to deal with situations where we are present, but it is this focus on bare emotions that enable us to get into the present. Other examples are meditating on the profundity of what it is we are about to talk to; visualising a powerful consensus outcome to the meeting; focusing on the other person's emotional state.

A mentor of mine, the very complex Geoff North would tell me that he could only conduct three coaching sessions per day. If you have been responsible for coaching executives you might relate to this. He says that the way in which he remains in the present is the reason that he cannot sustain it for more than a few hours each day. He focuses on achieving an outcome that is positive to the other person, to the exclusion of his own opinions, desires and feelings. His principle driver is one of servitude, he is entirely immersed in an emotional state, empathising with the coachee to help them solve and resolve their challenges. It's exhausting.

A colleague and friend who is a partner at a well-known legal practice is a terrific and formidable negotiator. He is able to come up with innovative solutions so quickly; he's one of those people that thinks of the right thing to say at the right time. Do you know people like that? Very frustrating for the rest of us that generally think of the right thing to have said once the moment has passed. His presence at negotiations is almost incandescent and I asked him how he managed to be so alive, so present; he said, *"I'm in the moment because I love negotiation."* He went on to explain, *"I have an outcome that I have to achieve and there's really no alternative and I'm really very confident that I have the right justification and all of the answers."*

Religious preachers often speak of being touched by the spirit when they are addressing a congregation. I imagine that politicians can feel that way too when they fervently believe in something too. I can relate to that, can you? Can you think of a time when you have been engaged in a conversation and felt totally alive and in the moment? If you can then ask yourself what it was that you were talking about. Was it something that you believed passionately about? Was it something inspiring that the other person was passionate about?

Summary

How will you get in the present, in the room? Is it laughter? A genuine yearning to resolve another's challenge? Finding something inspiring in the other's interest?

Conclusion

I started off this chapter introducing four ingredients that when added to your personal interactions will enable you to be present. I want to finish it by revisiting something else that I said earlier on. Imagine achieving a win-win outcome to a negotiation; securing buy-in from senior management; impressing on decision makers the importance of project management decision making.

If you believe that change is important and if you want to get involved in a revolution then get into being present, engaging with stakeholders, stepping in to their shoes, getting passionate about things, listening actively and maybe a bit of laughing in the mirror.

My final point is this, the most interesting person is often the most interested.

Lesson Twelve:

Be present in the present.

Chapter Fourteen. Embed the Change

I want to talk, in this final chapter, about practical things that can be done to enhance if not guarantee the chances of a successful transition, the effective embedding of change.

It has not always been this way, this focus on embedding the change. In fact I recall formative years of project management practice where the scope was tightly defined to the exclusion of post-implementation activities. In my telecoms experiences of the late nineties we were very much encouraged to create project documentation that would prove a conclusive delivery. In effect, that we had handed over the capability, proved that it worked to the correct specification and achieved sign-off and acceptance without any care for its application in the client environment.

In 2007 I had my first experience of a systems-based approach to changing this, with the change management teams of a major retail bank.

Case Study 33: Stick Ability

The background problem was simple and easy to relate to, the sheer volume of changes arriving at the user destination was so huge that only a small fraction was being embedded. In practice this meant that some branches or regions would be embracing changes wholesale, others piecemeal and others not at all. Subsequent changes were then built on to this unstable foundation creating a poor structure. The end users became at first frustrated, then sceptical and finally apathetic. In reality they were not listening and there was no real incentive or consequence for them to change.

The retail market's business improvement department recognised this and it fell to a senior change manager, Andrew, to establish new ways of working with the business and ways to increase the degree of acceptance.

"We have become very good at delivering projects," Andrew explains, *"but we have distanced ourselves from the business. You could describe us as a service provider like technology services or property services, we were certainly not focused on business change."*

The solution proved to be very easy to set up but not at all easy to implement.

To deliver lasting change requires the change to be put in place and held in place by people that have a stake in the problem and the solution.

Change managers were not completely inexperienced in supporting implementation, it was not unusual for a 'warranty period' to be extended to the business but this would generally cover mechanical failure of processes, equipment and systems.

Success involved changing the project methodology. First up, the word "project" would be replaced with the word "change" and the focus of all initiatives would rest on a successful embedding the outcome. Secondly a deliverable entitled "embedded change" would be added. Thirdly, crucially, the business would be invited to participate much earlier in the process, by helping to shape the solution.

The changes to practice and process were heralded as new ways of working, accompanied by a comprehensive training solution and supported by a top down management message proclaiming that challenging the process and the solution would be supported to ensure the successful embedding of change.

I observed this process for four years. During this time I can say that the professionalism of the change management teams were greatly enhanced and perceived. Change initiatives were better planned and each had an embedding deliverable. Other positive observations were as follows:

- o The end user community were involved in the UAT (user acceptance testing) design and delivery.

- o The change manager actively engaged with the business managers to transfer ownership of the outcomes and benefits.

- o There was a shift in mindset to become more agile when dealing with delivery and implementation.

- o Readiness reports and activities were implemented throughout the initiative.

I mentioned that implementation was not easy and in fact, it was ironic that the failure of the business to engage in sufficient numbers was where the greatest issues were experienced.

The changes were very well-intentioned, targeted and focused. It's hard to see how they could have been better designed however, it was the well-intentioned professionals creating a better environment for the change-weary business – that is where the issues grew.

In many cases the change teams were able to enfranchise the business managers and the end user community but in many others they were not. The reasons for these knock backs were varied but generally applied to the fact that the business had no stake in the process. In the abstract this is a semantic argument but in a practical sense where there are diverse pressures applied to business managers there remained the option to create distance from a solution in which there was no stake, regardless of the correctness of the solution.

In 2013 the organisation took the dramatic step to remove the change management function from the equation, instead putting the delivery of change in the hands of the business, supported by change professionals. This is ongoing and so I have no comments on how well it is progressing but it is certainly well-intentioned and in ensuring business ownership it does remove the age-old excuse, "It wasn't our change!"

The lessons that I draw from this story are:

o   If there is a party that will be responsible for accepting the outcome of my initiative, I need them enfranchised at a point that will enable them to commit.

o   Well-intentioned plans are great but ineffective unless they incorporate those who can positively or negatively influence their outcome.

Signposting

I watched Colin Powell speak. He's very interesting, engaging and organised. I can't honestly remember what he was talking about but I do remember him doing something very smart. From the moment that he took to the stage he held forward his agenda, an agenda that he contracted with us, the audience, at the beginning.

He started off by asking if we were willing to come on a journey with him, of course we agreed and then he asked if we would be willing to answer a question at the conclusion of the talk. We agreed.

He spoke for, probably, no more than 30 minutes but repeatedly he made reference to the journey and to the fact that he was approaching the point at which we would have to answer the question.

He provided us with measurable milestones, he would make five points at the conclusion of which he would ask us the question. At the end of each point he would summarise and tell us how many points out of five we had navigated and how many there were to go.

When the time came for the question, everyone knew it was coming, there were no surprises.

It's called signposting and it gives the audience comfort in knowing why they are there and what is expected of them. It was a nice touch asking the audience for permission, it created a contract and we were enfranchised in the talk.

Embedding change is quite similar in practice.

If we engage with the end users, ask them for permission, tell them what to expect, give them signposts and manage their expectations then there are no surprises. That's not to say that things won't go wrong because they will, it's just that we will be working together towards a mutually agreed and anticipated outcome and so resolving those issues will be much more easily navigated.

Unfreeze – change – freeze

The Kurt Lewin model for change, developed originally in the 1950s is a powerful and memorable approach to the complicated problem of cultural resistance, to which I referred in a previous chapter. At this final stage in the process and in the final chapter of the book I want to illustrate how central to change, stakeholder management is.

Lewin's model can be described with the following actions:

1. To unfreeze, it is necessary to create a desire to change, a vision of a brighter, better, necessary future state beyond the current one. There must first be a recognition that the status quo is not sustainable and that change is, at the least, desirable and at best, essential.

2. Changing or transitioning between the unfreezing and freezing points is the most delicate stage, at least for the recipients of change. At either end of the spectrum there is certainty and stability, in the middle is anxiety and uncertainty. It's like moving house; making the decision to move and putting the house on the market and selecting the new house, that is a difficult step for many; however, it is the uncertainty between exchange and completion and physically moving house that most will report as the stressful part. It's during this transition that information, access to support and visible leadership is essential to providing the comfort, certainty and security.

3. Freezing or re-freezing is the process or activities designed to ensure that the change sticks, that there is no regression and that the benefits are realised. Change professionals talk about removing alternatives and providing warranties, about training, process and operating models. There's no one true formula, rather a response to the feedback that is received from the business and a commitment to the change benefits.

Critics of the model point to the fact that re-freezing doesn't last long and that it is often compromised by new changes. I'll respond to this with an analogy. In the world of technology where organisations have multiple applications that interface and synchronise with each other there is an absolute necessity to evaluate the impact of changes to any one part of the architecture in order to maintain the integrity of the whole. In other words the upgrade to one application must not have a negative impact on any other application.

To this end the organisation will generally maintain two technology environments that are able to mirror the actual application relied upon by the business. Now this is the interesting part, one of the environments must always mirror exactly the production environment (platform *a*), the other less so (platform *b*). Any change is first tested on platform *a* to ensure that it performs as expected in isolation, interfacing as necessary with the other applications. Once this has been tested and proven the change is then uplifted to the second environment where its impact and effectiveness is tested against the entire architecture. If the change can be accommodated, often subject to small tweaks, it can be uplifted to the actual production environment. At this point platform *a* is updated so that subsequent changes are tested against the modified environment.

My point is that we can learn to ensure that the operating environment, the processes and practices of the business are built upon in a controlled manner and not subject to constant change.

I worked with a global outsourcing company for a few years. They had a reputation in practice for constantly changing people's job descriptions, responsibilities and roles. This worked very well for the entrepreneurial growth years but less well when customers and shareholders demanded reliability and predictability.

Lesson Thirteen:

Freeze and now relax.

The End

It's taken me a long time to finish this book. I've been to three different continents, met a thousand change, project and programme management professionals, spoken at conferences, been amazed by comments from change leaders and graduates alike. Change management is alive, it is diverse and it remains challenging and rewarding.

I believe that change management is a response to risk. My view of what change management is has been regularly challenged but I am very firm now on a definition that drives my beliefs about what good change management is. The thing that we, as change professionals, all agree on is that our raison d'etre is to respond to the risks of uncertainty, ambiguity and the unknown that are inherent in change. I believe that change management is a response to risk and I believe that one of the most significant risks is that the initiative to deliver the service, result, process or product is done without a guiding coalition of change and that the manifest outcome of this disconnect is friction, frustration and often failure.

If, at the concept stage of change, the risk assessment is highlighting a significant dependence on people to support, acknowledge, permit and accept the change then the change leader should be mitigating those risks; ensuring that the capability, the will and the energy required to gain and maintain a guiding coalition for change exists and is sustainable.

This book proposes tools and ingredients that can help bring about change when applied appropriately, I hope that you find it useful.

Lessons in Leadership

Lesson 1. Know your outcomes but know your risks better.

Lesson 2. Surround yourself with giants.

Lesson 3. Get a prescription.

Lesson 4. Hold high that umbrella.

Lesson 5. Look left and right before crossing the road.

Lesson 6. Get intimate with stakeholders.

Lesson 7. Clear the path.

Lesson 8. All stakeholders present and accounted for.

Lesson 9. Steer into the wind.

Lesson 10. Stand out from the crowd.

Lesson 11. See good, hear good, speak good.

Lesson 12. Be present in the present.

Lesson 13. Freeze and now relax.

Appendix: Tables, Figures and Case Studies

Tables

Figures

www.ajpconsulting.org

Case Studies